A LITTLE PIECE OF US -

It's Never Too Late to Be Creative.

By
The Pensmiths

Published by New Generation Publishing in 2020

Copyright © The Pensmiths 2020

First Edition

The author asserts the moral right under the Copyright, Designs and Patents Act 1988 to be identified as the author of this work.

All Rights reserved. No part of this publication may be reproduced, stored in a retrieval system or transmitted, in any form or by any means without the prior consent of the author, nor be otherwise circulated in any form of binding or cover other than that which it is published and without a similar condition being imposed on the subsequent purchaser.

ISBN
    Paperback   978-1-80031-485-6
    Ebook   978-1-80031-484-9

www.newgeneration-publishing.com

New Generation Publishing

This book has been supported by
The London Borough of Barking and
Dagenham Library Service - Pen to Print
Creative Writing Programme.
Pen to Print is funded by Arts Council,
England
as a National Portfolio Organisation.

Pen to Print
WHAT'S YOUR STORY?

Connect with Pen to Print
Email: pentoprint@lbbd.gov.uk
Web: pentoprint.org

Supported using public funding by
ARTS COUNCIL ENGLAND

Barking & Dagenham

CONTENTS PAGE

INTRODUCTION 1
ABOUT THIS BOOK 3
KATHY'S PROMPT 5
ABOUT KATHY 5
    KATHY'S 6
    BAILEY'S 9
    VICKI'S 12
    KEV'S 14
    JONATHAN'S 18
    MARK'S 20
    EMILY'S 22
    SKY'S 25
VICKI'S PROMPT 27
ABOUT VICKI 27
ABOUT BAILEY 27
    VICKI'S 28
    KEV'S 29
    JONATHAN'S 31
    MARK'S 33
    EMILY'S 34
    SKY'S 37
    KATHY'S 38
    BAILEY'S 40
    NATALIE'S 41

KEV'S PROMPT	43
ABOUT KEV	43
KEV'S	44
JONATHAN'S	45
MARK'S	47
EMILY'S	48
KATHY'S	49
BAILEY'S	51
VICKI'S	53
JONATHAN'S PROMPT	55
ABOUT JONATHAN	55
JONATHAN'S	56
MARK'S	57
EMILY'S	59
SKY'S	61
KATHY'S	63
BAILEY'S	64
VICKI'S	65
KEV'S	67
MARK'S PROMPT	71
ABOUT MARK	71
MARK'S	72
EMILY'S	73
SKY'S	76
KATHY'S	79
BAILEY'S	80

- VICKI'S 82
- KEV'S 85
- JONATHAN'S 87

EMILY'S PROMPT 89
ABOUT EMILY 89
- EMILY'S 90
- SKY'S 92
- KATHY'S 94
- BAILEY'S 95
- VICKI'S 97
- KEV'S 99
- JONATHAN'S 101
- MARK'S 102

SKY'S PROMPT 105
ABOUT SKY 105
- SKY'S 106
- KATHY'S 109
- BAILEY'S 111
- VICKI'S 113
- KEV'S 115
- JONATHAN'S 116
- MARK'S 119
- EMILY'S 120

NATALIE'S PROMPT 123
ABOUT NATALIE 123
- KATHY'S 124

- KEV'S 126
- JONATHAN'S 127
- MARK'S 129
- EMILY'S 130
- SKY'S 132

DANNY'S PROMPT 135
ABOUT DANNY 135
- DANNY'S 136
- BAILEY'S 138
- VICKI'S 139
- KEV'S 141
- JONATHAN'S 143
- MARK'S 145
- EMILY'S 147
- SKY'S 149
- KATHY'S 151

HANNAH'S PROMPT 153
ABOUT HANNAH 153
- HANNAH'S 154
- BAILEY'S 155
- VICKI'S 156
- KEV'S 157
- JONATHAN'S 158
- KATHY'S 159
- MARK'S 161
- EMILY'S 161

SKY'S	163
CESAR'S PROMPT	165
ABOUT CESAR	165
MARK'S	167
EMILY'S	168
SKY'S	170
BAILEY'S	172
VICKI'S	174
GISELLE'S PROMPT	177
ABOUT GISELLE	177
JONATHAN'S	178
MARK'S	179
EMILY'S	181
BAILEY'S	183
VICKI'S	184
KEV'S	187

INTRODUCTION

We are a writing group who meet weekly at our local community centre. We began as part of a Green Shoes Arts project, but when they could no longer fund our lovely facilitator, Natalie, we became independent; but with their continued support running in the background.

Our sessions consist of us dipping into our creativity to write short ten-minute pieces from a prompt. We don't worry about grammar, punctuation or presentation when we write during our sessions; it's about getting pen to paper and then reading our piece to the rest of the group. We come from all walks of life, and it amazes us at how diverse the pieces of writing are, considering that they come from the same prompt.

THE PENSMITHS

Mark Jones
Sky Kelly
Emily Khoury
Kathy Meade
Bailey Taylor
Victoria Taylor
Kev Walton
Jonathan Wright

And a contribution by our honorary members:
Natalie McMonagle
Danny Parker
Hannah Rowland

If you would like to contact us or would like to know about any Green Shoes Arts or Pen to Print projects, then email us at
pensmiths2018@outlook.com

ABOUT THIS BOOK

When we decided to create this book, each member supplied a prompt to the group, and then we all wrote a short piece of work for it. Each chapter in this book is a prompt; some are longer than others as members decided if they wished to contribute or not. Some of the members left the group without submitting any writing, but as we had already started the project, their prompts have been included.

As you read through, you will see that each of us write with our own style and we have taken the prompts in different directions. We hope that you enjoy our book.

KATHY'S PROMPT

THE HOLE IN THE WALL.

ABOUT KATHY

Kathy started writing at the age of 65, never having written anything before. She went on a four-week course at her local College, caught the writing bug, and now enjoys attending the weekly creative writing group.
She discovered a penchant for writing poetry and is now in the process of trying to write a book of her poems.
Now aged 71 she is living proof that you're never too old to learn.

KATHY'S

The cafe on the beach at Trethgowan had lain empty and neglected since old Mrs Tremayne had died some years back. With no one to inherit it, it now stood empty and forlorn, the once glossy for sale sign now tipsy and rusting in the salty sea air.

When Sally and Rob moved back to her childhood home after Rob's redundancy, Sally was determined to show him the place which held so many happy memories from her youth. She recalled long hot summers when she had helped in the thriving cafe serving the ever-popular homemade food cooked lovingly by Mrs Tremayne.

Locals and tourists alike would flock to try her famous cakes and scones. When Mrs Tremayne had noticed Sally's interest in cooking, she had taken her under her wing and taught her everything she knew, and when Sally completed her course at Catering College, Mrs Tremayne had been the first to congratulate her.

Soon after the family had moved to London and Sally's memories of the old cafe had receded with time. But now when Sally saw the cafe, her heart leapt.

"We could afford this with your redundancy pay," she said to Rob.

"You must be joking! There's so much to be done; we could never afford to do it up."

"We could all chip in and do the work. I'm sure it's worse than it looks," pleaded Sally.

"Once we're up and running and with my baking and your Mum helping, we could invest the profits back into the business. And there's the big flat at the back; we wouldn't have to pay rent out."

Rob knew when he was beaten and, two months later, paperwork completed, they stood outside their new premises. Sally's brother Tim and his wife had come down to help, and so the work began stripping down the walls and dismantling the old shelving. It was as Rob pulled down the counter at the back that he saw it. A great big gaping hole in the wall.

"Look at this Sal. I wonder what's behind this?" Placing his hand inside he felt a large door handle.

"It's only a partition wall," said Tim. "Let's knock it down and see what's there."

They removed the plasterboard to reveal a massive wooden door.

"How strange! Is there a key?" asked Sally.

"Nothing in the lock," said Rob. "Pass a torch and let's have a closer look."

"There's something down there on the floor," said Tim. "It's a key; it must have been lying there for goodness knows how long." After quite a few tugs and turns the door finally creaked open to reveal a long black tunnel.

"Let's take a look," said Rob. As they ventured further, the tunnel widened until they found themselves in a cave which opened onto a sandy cove.

"We're in Trethgowan bay," said Sally to Rob as they stepped out into the bright sunlight. "Me and Tim used to play here as children."

A shout from the cave drew their attention back inside. Tim and Marie motioned them over to a large black box hidden behind some rocks. As Rob opened the creaking lid, he gasped in surprise.

"It's gold coins and jewellery! Wouldn't like to guess how long it's been here."

"Hells Bells!" said Sally, "What should we do with it?"

"We have to tell the Police, I suppose," replied Rob.

As they showed the coins to Sergeant Collins in the local Police Station and related the story, he looked at them in disbelief.

"How many did you say?" he asked.

"There's a whole boxful of gold pieces and other gold trinkets," said Sally.

"We'll need to investigate further, leave it to me," replied the officer.

Some weeks later, as Sally and Rob had nearly finished the refurbishing of the café, Sergeant Collins appeared with a sheaf of papers.

"We've done some research and spoken to an expert, and there's an incredible story behind this. Apparently, this cove was once the main hub for pirates to hide their stolen loot. In 1664 a ship named The Carolina was wrecked off this coast. It was a mystery at the time, and, according to our expert, the ship simply vanished with no trace. None of it was ever seen again. We've examined the box, and there are some markings on the underside with the ships name which confirms the box came from there."

"The good news," the Sergeant continued, "is that you are entitled to claim all the contents. Just sign these papers for me, and it's all yours."

A few days later, Sally and Rob stared at each other in amazement as the specialist coin dealer told them the value of the coins. With the unexpected windfall, they were able to buy expensive furniture and finish the work to a higher standard and pride of place was the large sign over the door in blue and gold lettering. THE HOLE IN THE WALL CAFE.

"I think it's the only name we could call it, don't you think?" smiled Rob.

BAILEY'S

Rosie is bursting with excitement as she opens the door to her first ever house. It's an old Victorian house that has an eerie sense, but Rosie sees the spacious rooms as the place which will become her home and later on protect her family that she wishes to have. She sighs as she slowly shuts the door behind her and her mother, Charlie.

"So mum, what do you think?" she shyly asks.

"Rosie, it's beautiful. I can see why you love it. We can easily turn this into a comfy home." Charlie smiles.

"Let's get on with it then!" Rosie laughs.

The two of them get to work on the aged wallpaper as it's not what Rosie had in mind. After hours of work in the living room and the downstairs bathroom and several tea breaks, they began to tackle the hallway. Rosie peels back piece by piece of wallpaper, an action that quickly became tedious when she came across a small slit in the wall.

"Mum, where's the filler gone? There's a gap that needs filling," Rosie asked. This prompted Charlie to come to take a look, which led to a bewildering discovery.

"Rosie, it's a keyhole. Have you seen a key about?"

They have a rummage around in several kitchen and hallway drawers until an old, rusted key is found, and with the rest of the wallpaper removed, Rosie puts the key in and turns it with anticipation. Charlie, with the expectation of a basement, and Rosie, with the dream of a goldmine, they enter the room. Disappointment fell upon both of their faces. A room with nothing but an old wardrobe in the corner is what they faced.

"That's one more piece of furniture we need to get rid of," Charlie sighed, clearly knowing the charge of a removal van.

The warm evening glow begins to fade, and Charlie decides that it's time to leave her daughter in her new home. Rosie climbs the creaky stairs to where she has already placed her double bed. She falls lightly into a blissful sleep, but then she's suddenly woken by a strange sound that echoes around her empty house. Intrigued, along with a feeling of anxiousness, Rosie rises out of her bed to go and investigate. It's early morning so she can see well, so she follows the sound of scraping like a sharp object against drywall, a sound she became familiar with that day as she scraped wallpaper with her tool.

The subtle sound has led her to the newly discovered room which she recalls she locked before bed. Curiosity fights off her fear as she slowly opens the door, which loudly creaks. She breathes slowly and steadily until she can clearly see the room. She steps further into the room, and she doesn't notice anything different, so she turns to leave with a sigh of relief. But as she turns, she is surprised with a gruesome sight. Written upon the wall in what she can only assume is blood is the words, 'LEAVE WHILE YOU STILL CAN.'

She hurries out the room, and with two shaky hands, she locks the door and phones the police, followed by her mum. As the police arrive, she opens the door again, just for the officers to report that there's no writing on the wall, let alone any blood.

"Rosie. It must be because you're unsure of living by yourself. Come home, we can still decorate, but until we're done, stay with me."

"Mum, I have to do this. Obviously, I'm just a little on edge as this is all new, go home. I'm sorry for calling you here," Rosie says, sheepishly.

Putting the mornings' events behind her, Rosie went out to pick up some paint to cover her bare walls. She returns home, feeling excited again to fulfil her dream, to find the nightmare door to be slightly open. Rosie curses under her breath as she remembers that she didn't make sure that the police locked it after their brief investigation. She checks her watch and works out that her mum will be over in 3 hours to help her paint, so she decides to get the place prepared. She heads up the stairs to grab some old bedsheets to cover the wooden floors with, but then she hears some heavy footsteps climbing the stairs and her body freezes. She slowly turns to face her bedroom door, once again cursing, as she left her phone downstairs, and she meets her fate. The face that appears is not a face at all, just a sheet of white and holes where eyes should be. The figure's hands weren't hands but long sharp spears that now scrape across the floor, teasing Rosie, as she knew that she'd soon feel the full impact of them on her skin.

Charlie unlocks the front door and calls out her daughter's name. A lack of reply made her heart full as the memories of the morning rush back. Instantly she checks in the room that started this fear, but there was no sign of life, just the wardrobe staring back at her. Now, almost reluctantly, she ventures upstairs to where she's imaging Rosie taking a nap on her bed.

But that's not what she finds. A heart-breaking scream erupts through the house as Charlie holds the lifeless body of her daughter.

On the wall behind the bed, a message was written: 'YOU WERE WARNED.'

A quick sample will match the red words to the blood of Rosie's.

VICKI'S

The castle stood tall and proud atop the steep hill. Being nearly 500 years old, it had seen many a season come and go. Tree's, once just seeds, have fought each other for the prime position, reaching towards the sky and are now centuries old. One of the twin towers no longer stood, the other alone now standing guard in a world that it no longer served a purpose in.

Centuries ago its halls were visited by Kings and Queens; its walls were roamed by men-at-arms keeping guard against the possible onslaught of an enemy army. The moat was filled with dark, deep waters, and the kitchens were filled with many a servant at work to keep their employer fed and happy.

Now, the halls were roamed by paying guests eager to get a glimpse of how the dead once lived, the pitted and scarred walls are used to look at the fantastic views that could be seen from its heights. The moat is dry and covered in grass and families now sit there to take a rest or lay out their picnic baskets for lunch. The kitchens now have the pots and pans displayed in cabinets, no longer serving a purpose and the embers in the firepit have long grown cold.

The storeroom once home to the castle supplies wherein the only noises heard would be the giggles from a serving girl as she sneaked to meet her lover, had now been butchered and changed to accommodate a castle shop and café.

Screams were still heard from deep down the in the dungeon, but whereas the cries of the past were painfilled and from the dying; now they were from children as their dads jump out to scare them in the dark, chilly room. The things that the walls had witnessed from the past have been soaked up; the memories from the dead call out to the living as they brush their hands along the bricks. Those hairs that stand up on the back of their necks as they imagine what life must have been like for those being tortured were the hands of the past being outstretched, imploring for release.

Long ago, the castle wall was complete and unbreeched. But for centuries now there has been a hole in the wall. A mother now sits on its broken, jagged edge; she is taking photos of her children as they run and play chase. They are wild and carefree enjoying their fantastic day out, even the older child has forgotten his gadgets and is running free with his siblings. Her heart swells as she watches them, not a care in the world.

The day that that hole in the wall was created saw another boy, similar in age standing with the older men and boys in the courtyard; the castles last line of defence. He held a sword too heavy for him, wearing mismatched armour that served no purpose that just weighed him down. His eyes looked up to the internal wall and found those of his mother. They spoke no words; their goodbyes had already been spoken.

Suddenly the wall is blown in, and she loses sight of her boy in the mass of bodies that surge over the wall. She can't help herself as she runs, runs, runs to find him, as she hears metal clang against metal and the sound of people dying fills the air. She makes it to the hole, but before she gets over the rubble, she feels a burning, sharp pain and she looks down at her chest at the arrow sticking out. She died not knowing how her son fared.

So, as the mother stands watching her children play, another mother, unseen and centuries old, looks across an ancient battlefield. She prays that her son will one day be found amongst the bones of the dead, the broken swords, arrowheads and dented armour that now make up the uneven grass-covered ground long ago buried beneath the feet of the living.

But the present soon becomes the past, another day passes, and this castle is the place where history lives.

KEV'S

Santa Claws

1996, Sarah's bedroom, Christmas eve.

"Mum look there's a hole in my wall," said Sarah, aged eleven.

"That's not a hole; it's a little bit of paint chipped off. Have you got a poster I could put over it?" answered her mum Julie

"Yeah, put my big Grinch poster over it."

Julie put the poster over the hole and kissed her daughter goodnight.

"What about me?" shouted out Julie's other daughter, Amy who was twelve from her room.

"I'm coming," she shouted back.

1998, Amy's bedroom, Christmas eve.

"Mum, I have a hole appearing in my wall!" yelled Amy, aged fourteen.

Julie came and looked and saw a very small hole.

"No prob," she said, "have you got a poster I could put over it?"

"I've got that big picture of the Krampus film," Amy replied.

Julie put it up over the hole.

2002, front room of the family home, Christmas eve.

Decorations adorn the walls, stockings hang on the mantelpiece, and a large tree full of tinsel and baubles sits in the corner.

"I wish Dad were here," whispered Sarah. Dad was Corporal Stanley Tomlin, serving in the army and not being allowed to come home this year, because he was in Syria.

"He will phone first thing in the morning," came the reply from Amy.

In the background on the T.V was a documentary about murders that happened previously on Christmas. Mum got the remote and turned it off.

"Okay girls, time for bed," mum said.

Both girls arose and kissed their mother goodnight, then went to their rooms.

2002 Sarah's bedroom.

Sarah awoke, sure she heard a noise; a soft ripping sound floated by on the night air. She got up and slipped on her slippers, and she proceeded to her Mums room. Upon entering the room, Sarah saw the lamp on and a splattering of red stains on the walls, she approached the wall and saw it was blood.

She looked to the left of the bed and noticed her mum, sliced from naval to the neck, her intestines were sitting on the floor next to her. She let out a silent scream, not wanting to alert anybody if they were still in the house

Sarah quickly and quietly tiptoed to Amy's room, tears streaming down her face. Amy's door was ajar, she peeped through the doorjamb, but could not see anything. The sound had turned from a ripping noise to a slurping one. In the corner of the room, she saw a figure, not being able to see properly, she turned the light on.

The figure was big; very big, with long dirty hair, fingernails at least eight inches in length, with sharp-pointed tips. His face was scarred from head to jaw, and he appeared to be naked. Sarah just had time to scream out loud when she saw what the thing was eating; her sisters now hollow stomach. It leapt at her before she could move an inch, the sharp nails ripped her nightdress, and a slice of her breast opened as her blood sprayed everywhere.

Sarah turned and ran, but the figure was fast, it grabbed her and threw her across the room. Her head hit the side of the dressing table, and her eyes blurred. Its face came right up to Sarah's and started to sniff. It sniffed her belly and chest and her hair. The tongue flickered out of its gnarly mouth and began to lick

Sarah's face. Her eyes were shut tightly, and she smelt his foul odour, and its tongue felt as rough as sandpaper.

Sarah stayed still for what seemed like hours, slowly she opened her eyes and the figure had gone. She moved in slow motion, taking ages to reach the door. The television was back on, the light from it sending dancing shadows down the hallway and a voice could be heard saying,

'A creature that attacked and killed women every Christmas, since 1992. A girl that survived the first attack described the figure as the one who had killed her mum and sister.'

Sarah crept to the end of the hall, and she saw the figure sitting watching the news. He sat motionlessly. Sarah was sweating and breathing heavy as she tried to control her body.

As she was about to move, a creepy booming voice whispered. "Hi, I am known as Santa Claws; instead of bringing presents, I take mine."

Immediately he pogo'ed up and with a wave of his hand, sliced Sarah's throat. She gargled and dropped to the floor as her blood ran down her body.

Santa Claws licked his lips and jumped on her, opening up her belly, and he started eating.

"Merry Christmas Mum," he uttered as he started on her womb.

JONATHAN'S

Long ago, perhaps in a time when you had not yet been born, there were no cashpoint machines. If you wanted money for the weekend, you had to go to the bank on Friday. The banks closed at 3.30 and were always busy in the afternoon. If you worked 9-5, it was not always convenient to go in the morning, and you could spend your lunchtime queuing and then having to go back to work without the extra money.

If you hadn't judged your finances correctly, you could find yourself broke until Monday morning, when you joined a lot of other people in the same predicament.

Thank God for cashpoint machines, even those charging £1.95 a time. I don't like the latter as I tend to take out a lot more than the usual £20 or £30 and worry about whether I'll be mugged before I spend it.

I think about my trials and tribulations as I wait for the woman in front of me to complete her transaction. Luckily for me, the machine is functional. I can't stand it when I queue for ages, and the machine has run out of money. I have never seen anyone filling up a machine. I suppose they do it via the back — much less risk. The money is probably delivered by a Securicor van, and the contents will blow up if someone tampers with the back door. What a waste of money, but I don't suppose that the KLF would care. As so much money is wasted in the UK, I guess a few thousand pounds exploding in a van won't make much difference.

I take my debit card out of my wallet and key in the code 9999. I wonder how many people would work that one out. I prefer calling it the code, rather than the

PIN number as Personal Identification Number Number is a load of rubbish, as far as I'm concerned.

My code is accepted, and I ask for £20 and hope that I get a tenner and two fivers, rather than a £20 note. I find those so difficult to spend if I want to buy a cheap item.

"There are insufficient funds in your account."

I thought I had topped up my account recently, but the bank is shut. I try to phone the emergency number, but my mobile's battery is dead.

I look back at the screen.

"Would you like some emergency funds?"

Arrows were pointing to 'Yes' and 'No'. I pressed 'Yes' and chose to take out £50.

"Would you like help, so you never get into debt again?"

This was too good to be true. I pressed 'Yes' again.

There was a whooshing sound as a gust of wind left the machine and permeated my body, tearing my soul apart.

I am now inside the machine, and I'm looking through the slot at the next customer. My former body has retrieved my card and my £50 and has walked away. He will never be in debt again if the oracle's claims are to be believed.

I wait inside the cashpoint for another client with insufficient funds to pay their bills. It is only then that I can be complete again, but whose body I shall enter remains to be seen.

MARK'S

After three years, Mary finally plucked up the courage to go to the hole. It had appeared from nowhere, and the tales she had heard couldn't all be true. Today was her turn, and she felt a little bit excited about the experience.

After a long drive, she arrived at the hole and as she stared into it, a face peered back. It was as if she was looking into a mirror, then before she could act, an arm pulled her into the hole, and she was now on the other side. She looked through and the 'other' her was talking, but the only word she could lip-read was 'home'.

She screamed, 'Come back!' to the other her, but she was gone. Mary had to go home, she sees her car there, and the keys were still in it, and a strip of something with 'Touch this!' written above it. She does, and a flood of memories hit her like bullets in her mind. She is a bit dazed, but she goes home, and as she walks through the doorway a flash of memories hit her; a wedding, her high-school sweetheart Frank, and their two children Sarah and Geoff. Both have left home now. In her own home, she'd never had children as she'd never recovered from Franks death in a car crash. She wanted to go back home, but part of her wanted to stay.

A week passed, and with the memory flashes, she got through it. She went to the hole every day to look for her doppelgänger, hoping to return home. All she sees today is a dog standing, chained up near the hole. She gets an idea; she grabs the dog and pulls him through but keeps the chain on the other side, so if needed, she can get back there. When she looks at her home tears start to appear, it was a mess! Buildings were destroyed, smoke filled the air, and most noticeably of all, empty streets. There was not a soul, just a letter with 'Mary' on it taped to a lamppost. She opened the letter and read it.

Dearest Mary,

Sorry for the lack of a letter on the other side but I know, as you are me, your tenacious and would not believe me, so I needed you to see this. Your world is gone; destroyed by war. Everyone you knew and loved here are gone.

I searched for you for a long time on someone who's world was doomed. You see, I am dying, and I have not the strength or courage to tell my family. I can't leave them alone, so I found you. Please forget this place and look after my family. They need me, well, us. Being here, I see that Frank died and that you never got the life I did. For you going through that, I am really sorry. I've had many great years with him now it's your turn to have some good times with him.

Thank you, and again please look after them.

Mary.

Mary was sad. She wanted the life so bad but wasn't sure if she deserved it. A second chance with her Frank! She sits there for a good hour and then decides to go back to her new family where she made loads of good memories; she even had a child of her own, a girl called Martha after her mum. She lived the life that the other Mary had wanted.

Now it was that years had passed, and Mary was at the end. Frank had died two years ago, and she was ready. She read the letter to her family, who all laughed it off as her having one last laugh with them. She turns, closes her eyes and slowly goes to meet her maker, knowing her last act was making her family laugh.

EMILY'S

It was a fascinating dream. When Alice woke up, she wrote all about it before forgetting the details. Many days after it was still on her mind and thoughts of how strange yet wonderful it was.

One day as Alice went for a walk, she changed her usual route of walking into town along the coastal path and turned to the opposite direction. The whole area was still new to her as only six months had passed since moving into a quaint little thatched cottage. It was a delight having both countryside and coast so near to her new home.

After twenty minutes she saw a sign on the left of the road saying Old Manor House. Intrigued, she followed the arrow and came upon the house. It looked empty with bare filthy windows and one broken.

She walked all the way around the house marvelling at the architecture and wondering why it had been left empty and now in a state of disrepair. When at the back of the house she noticed a hole in the wall with ivy trailing around it. Suddenly, her strange dream of late came to mind.

"I wonder," she said out loud as seized by an impulse to climb through the hole, just big enough for her size. "Carp Diem," she muttered, feeling like a child on an adventure.

When through she sat down on the grass which was richly decorated with buttercups, daisies and other wildflowers names of which she didn't know. While looking around, she sensed that she was not alone. Feeling uneasy with thoughts of running away when suddenly she heard a tiny voice saying "There you are Alice. It's alright, don't be frightened. We have been expecting you."

She looked around, yet no one was there!

"Am I losing my marbles she uttered?"

"No Alice, no lost marbles, look down."

Oh, my goodness you would have to have been there to believe it. As the saying goes, seeing is believing.

Continue reader if you are gripped with Alice's adventure as there's more, there's more.

Alice looked down and what she saw made her rub her eyes a few times to make sure she was seeing straight. Two tiny little people stood to her left near her feet. One was dressed in sky-blue t-shirt and red trousers with a full head of curly ginger hair. The other was dressed in a red and green checked dress, with ribbons adorning her plaited blond hair.

Alice gasped, putting her hand over her mouth as the little man said, "Hi Alice, we have been expecting you."

"What, expecting me; why?" asked Alice.

"Your dream last week was our prompt to you. Now you are here, we are so delighted, Alice. We have chosen you as our human helper in return for membership to our village. My name is Alfonzo, Chieftain of our village and this is my beautiful wife, Isobel."

Alice rubbed her eyes again, sure that she was daydreaming. No, it was happening for real.

"Come have tea cake and meet the others." That said, Alice tentatively followed them across an overgrown path.

Five minutes later, a beautiful tree house appeared in front of her.

"This is our entrance and look-out post."

Many hours passed and Alice had been introduced to all the fairies. Alfonzo and Isobel insisted she sit between them as villagers chatted to her with smiles on their faces.

"Will you consider our offer, Alice?" asked Alfonzo.

"To be honest, this needs further consideration," replied Alice. With that, she said, "Farewell, for now, I will return in seven days to give you my answer."

Alice was escorted back to the hole in the wall waving goodbye to all and sauntered home to her cottage.

It would be a leap in faith if she took up the fairies' proposition. However, mulling over her dream, then meeting the fairies, her decision was made. On the seventh day, Alice returned as promised to the old manor house.

Within a minute, Alfonzo appeared. "Hi Alice, well, don't keep us in suspense, my new friend."

"Hi Alfonzo, yes, yes for sure, let's do it," she grinned.

From that moment on time passed quickly. Alice sold her bungalow and bought the manor house. Within six months renovated and ready, the towns first nursery was opened in the manor. Alice lived upstairs, which was cornered off from the public. It had been a lonely dilapidated house and garden for many years. It was now a successful, thriving, lively, happy environment that the fairies had longed for.

Unbeknown to all except Alice, the only person with the gift of seeing the fairies. The nursery was open four days a week. The fairies were ecstatic. Alice was delighted and content with her leap of faith decision in moving forward on a new adventure.

As for seeing fairies, oh gosh, you would have to be there to believe it. So, so very magical.

SKY'S

I quickly ducked
as my brother threw the ball,
it zoomed past me
aiming at the wall.

I was winding him up
and he got mad,
he's not a good thrower
for that I'm glad.

It bounced off the wall
with a huge smack,
hitting him in the face
knocking him back.

He falls to the floor
staring at the ceiling,
are you okay?
I asked while kneeling.

His look was stern
followed by heaving breathing,
little hands making a fist
he was seething.

As we looked at the wall
the sight that greeted us,
a large crack glared
you know mum will make a fuss.

Just cover it up
and it'll be fine,
that's because you won't be in trouble
you annoying swine.

VICKI'S PROMPT

YOUR HOUSE LIGHTS GO OUT FOR TEN SECONDS. WHEN THEY COME BACK ON, THERE IS A NOTE STUCK TO YOUR WINDOW. IT SAYS JUST TWO WORDS, "RUN, NOW!"

ABOUT VICKI

I've had a love for reading and writing since I was little, but it has only been since attending the Pensmiths that I've grown in confidence in regard to what I write. In 2017, I achieved my lifelong ambition of seeing my work in print when my debut crime book, Haven, was published. I even have an author website now!

I take pleasure in introducing you to the youngest member of our group, Bailey. She is my daughter and attends our sessions during the school holidays. Unfortunately, she doesn't have a chapter, but she has submitted a piece to each prompt.

ABOUT BAILEY

I joined this writing group as I was encouraged to come along by my mum (Vicki), and I ended up enjoying the challenge of using prompts. Most of my creative writing occurs when I attend the group as I'm currently studying for my A-levels; therefore, I don't have a lot of spare time.

VICKI'S

Peter ran down into an alley that led to his street and checked behind him again. He hadn't heard any footsteps following, or cars slowing, so he hoped that meant that he had not followed him.

He got to the end of the alley and paused to catch his breath 'I'm getting too old for this spy game,' he thought. He touched his ear and twiddled his earpiece. He hadn't heard anything but static from it for a good few minutes now, and Peter hoped that his fellow agent, Derek, had safely left the area of their failed operation.

He was only a few houses away from his place when he suddenly heard a voice in his ear, making him jump,

"Mission is a fail. Your cover is blown!" shouted Derek. "Get away from here as fast as you can."

Those words are what every agent hopes that they will never hear; cover blown! Peter knew that he was in trouble and that he only had a little bit of time to get what he needed.

He had been working undercover for several months infiltrating Bedell's drug ring efficiently and slowly gaining their trust. Tonight was meant to be the big one. He was due to meet the head of the Bedell family, after which he knew that he would be ready to start the takedown. He would be privy to all the information he needed; he was so close to bringing the whole organisation down, frustratingly close!

Peter fumbled for his door keys, got inside and kicked the door closed behind him. He ran into the through lounge, reluctantly flicking the lights on as he passed the switch and went to his old-fashioned dresser unit where he had hidden away his real passport and a stash of cash.

All the time, he had questions running around in his head. How had it all gone wrong? How had they found out who he was? Is someone dirty in his department? Had he accidentally given himself away?

He had arrived at the meeting place, and things just hadn't felt right. Instinct and years of experience had kicked in, and Peter had turned and walked away, and as he did, he had heard a gunshot and a ping on a nearby wall. He hadn't waited around to give them another chance to hit him; Peter had fled.

While he was reaching behind the mirror in the dresser the lights suddenly went out, and ten seconds later they turned back on, straight away Peter's eyes were drawn to a piece of paper that had been put on his front window. There were two words written on it; "RUN, NOW!"

Peter felt like his heart was pumping in his mouth and fear held him stock still for a second. He forced himself to turn back to the dresser, and it was then that he saw a reflection of someone in the mirror. Peter's last thought was, "Too late!"

KEV'S

This bloody storm, three days it's been raging, the persistent rain and grey skies are having a severe effect on my two daughters. They keep telling me how bored they are and being cooped up inside is making them very cranky. It has only been four months since they lost their mother to the dreaded cancer.

The house lights keep flickering, and the noises from the house are scaring them, I always tell them mum is looking down and protecting them. Out of nowhere, the back door blows open with a loud thud, and rain pours in. I run to shut the door and wipe up the wet, and as I do so, the lights go out and don't come back on straight away.

Screams pierce the evening air, and after what seems like an eternity, the lights come back on. My two daughters run to cuddle me, still crying. As they get near, they both freeze, mouths open in fear, staring at the kitchen window. Written in the condensed air on the window are the words RUN NOW!

I stayed still mystified, after a minute or so I collected my thoughts and pick up both girls and run upstairs. When we reach the top stair, a crashing sound fills the air. I tell the girls to stay where they are as I go and investigate. I reach the kitchen door and see the giant oak tree that was once in the garden, now laying in what was left of my kitchen.

I go back to the girls and tell them to pack some clothes because we are going to stay in the local hotel.

When we came together in the upstairs hallway, I noticed 'RUN NOW!' written on the window. I grabbed the girls and told them to run for the car. We get to the bottom of the stairs near the front door when all hell breaks loose. The whole house shakes, and debris starts to shower down on us. I shove the girls outside and pogo out myself, just before the house crumbles down. I rush them to the car as a wall of dust comes at us.

Sitting in the car completely silent, we watch as the dust envelops us and the surrounding landscape. Both my daughters are crying and holding each other, so I climb in the back and hold them both tightly.

It seemed like we all fell asleep because upon opening my eyes, my youngest was whispering, "Please leave us alone".

I looked at the side window and I saw 'RUN NOW!'

'Not again,' I thought to myself. I awoke my eldest, and we all got out of the car, we were about fifty feet from the car when it catches fire, and it explodes.

I sat on the grass verge with a daughter either side; the chaos in front of us was like something out of an action film. We were all drained and breathless. I was grateful we are all still alive. But who did the warnings come from?

A bright light appeared in front of us, and both daughters looked up and seemed to smile at the same time. I squinted my eyes and noticed a figure in the light. The girls shouted out in unison, "Mum", and ran to the figure. I blinked not believing what I was seeing. Standing in front of us was Jay, my dead wife.

She scooped the girls in her arms and said, "I haven't got long, but I am here always to protect you. Just look up and call my name. I saw this accident happening and had to intervene, I'm sorry, but I have to go now".

As she faded back into the light, she said she loved and missed us all. We sat sobbing, tears running down our faces of loss and joy. For the rest of our lives, it did seem like we had our own guardian angel.

JONATHAN'S

YOUR HOUSE LIGHTS GO OUT...

Why do the lights go out when it is very dark, not when I can easily find my way to the fuse box? It takes me 10 seconds to find the fuse box, flick the switch and turn on the lights, apart from a faulty bulb.

That's strange. There's a note stuck to my window. How did that get there, and what does it mean? "RUN, NOW!"

How did my messenger get up to the 22nd floor of my tower block? What am I supposed to run from?

There is a banging noise downstairs. I don't know what it is, but it sounds threatening. Perhaps whoever or whatever it is will come for me next.

I open my front door and get into the lift. At least it will give me some breathing space, so I can work out what to do. Perhaps the fire escape will be the best route. I can hear people screaming as I move slowly upwards.

The lift doors open at the top floor. I walk along the corridor. I've never been here before. There has never been a reason to do so. The first few flats look very similar to the ones on my floor. There are a few variations, like doorbells and security gates. As I walk along, I see that the flats have turned into old-fashioned houses. Some of them have red crosses on their doors. I don't know if the colour is produced by blood or paint, but it looks creepy. I hear screams and sobs from inside the houses, and I feel scared. I pass the last house and find that I am walking along a dirt track and there are dead bodies all around. The trees have notices attached to the bark. "RUN, NOW!"

I see a priest by a boundary stone. He says, "You can go no further. Look into the stream."

I see purple blotches all over my face.

The priest continues, "We must ensure that the plague doesn't spread to other villages."

"Is there any means of escape?"

"Not for you."

MARK'S

When the lights come back on, I see two words 'Run, now!'

Jill, David and Katie run like hell not realising until it was far behind them that Paul was dead.

"My boy!" Jill screamed. They were so confused. What's going on? They all screamed, and then the lights go out again. They run about like mad and then the lights come back on. The words say, 'go left.'

David and Katie run and go left. Jill was now dead. They have some time to catch their breath, and they both cry, 'What the hell is going on here?' They scream as the lights go out again, and the message this time said, 'Stay here.' There was only Katie left now, and she thinks, 'There is no way I'm staying here!' She runs, and the door opens; she is free. She runs to the police as fast as she can.

She tells the police all about what happened, and they offer her some cocoa. They then take her back and much to her surprise the door is shut, and when they knock, Frank answers the door alive and well. Katie is in shock.

"We were told that you and your family died sir," the officer said.

Frank laughed, 'We have just come back from holiday,' he said, and then they all come out to prove that they are ok. The police have a few words with Katie, and she goes back to her family.

She enters the house and eats dinner, and then after dinner, the lights go off. When they come back, a sign appears saying 'Run.' Katie and Paul say 'Nope!' and they sit and watch TV. Her family run, and one by one, they come back to the living room. A few hours later, the police are at the door with David, and the pattern continues until they all ignore the note. The notes stop. What was going on? Who was leaving the notes, and why were they all not dead? The answer was simple; they were all in hospital from some illness from the holiday that they had been on and the whole thing was part of Katie's dream, and well, not all dreams are happy ones.

EMILY'S

It was a bitter winters night in November, and Jim had just arrived home cold and jaded from working a double shift, due to a shortage of staff. He turned the lights and heating on and went into the kitchen to prepare his dinner. He was looking forward to a comforting hot meal while watching television before retiring for a well-earned night's sleep.

Five minutes late, the lights went off, coming back on after a few moments. Jim turned around to get a pot from the cupboard and spotted a note stuck to the window. Putting his reading glasses on, he read the note, which said "RUN NOW" with a smiley emoji in bold red letters.

"Oh, shit! What the heck is this about?" he said out loud.

Jim momentarily wondered if a mate was pulling his leg and reminding him of his goal. For the last two months, he had been in training for an upcoming marathon. Being unfit and new to running, he had exercised daily plus going for a run around the local park.

Well reader, what would you do?

Jim turned off the stove, picked up his keys, mobile and coat, and with his hands shaking, he opened the front door and dashed up the road. He reached the bus stop just in time to board a bus that was about to drive off.

His hands and knees were shaking, his mind in a turmoil as instinctively he guessed who had left the note.

Knowing exactly what to do, he got off the bus ten minutes later and walked a further five minutes where he knew the police station was situated. Explaining his predicament to an officer, he was advised to stay put while they carried out an investigation.

Many hours passed as he sat in a side room alone before being informed that fingerprints had been taken from the note, windowpane and his kitchen. A suggestion was made that he stays away from his home until further notice.

So, Jim rang his sister Chloe asking if he could stay over for a few days.

"Of course, bro, no problem, see you soon."

He was then given a police escort and driven to her home 20 miles away. Jim told Chloe that he had a burst pipe indoors, flooding the downstairs area plus no electricity. She believed him, as no reason not to. He didn't want to freak her out by telling her his gut feeling. He knew he had taken a risk a few years ago with his actions.

Remembering a so-called friend who had bragged to him in the pub one evening, asking if he wanted in on a lucrative business. Adding sarcastically, was he man enough to ditch a low paid job for easy money?

On hearing what the business entailed, Jim was gobsmacked yet didn't show it. Not only was Andy growing hemp in his greenhouse, but he was also in receipt of a regular supply of cocaine. All to be sold on the open market to interested customers. In a reserved, calm manner, Jim said he would give it some thought and get back to him. Andy handed him a business card with his new address, and phone number saying, "Don't leave it too long otherwise, I'll hook up with another mate."

Jim then left the pub, knowing what course of action he would take. He was an upstanding, law-abiding citizen with zero tolerance for illegal drugs, let alone smuggling and selling them. He knew in his heart the truthful way ahead for himself and his conscience. That is why he went straight to the police station and nervously related his information.

After investigations fingerprints belonging to Andy were found in his home, resulting in his arrest the following morning. Jim knew that Andy had been released from prison recently and had felt a tad edgy at times, leading him to the police station after reading the note, sensing it wasn't a reminder from a mate to prepare for his marathon.

Jim was a witness in court as Andy was tried, sentenced and sent to jail. What ensued was Jim hearing through the grapevine Andy's reaction to his betrayal and a future plan of revenge.

So, reader, it wasn't rocket science Jim deducing who the note was from. The police were very supportive and didn't take the threat lightly, due to the fact Andy had served a prison sentence for attempted murder. So, he is back in prison for threatening behaviour and evidence found in his home that he had returned to drug dealing on release from prison.

SKY'S

BANG

"Finally! I'm home!" I couldn't help but kick the door open as I came home from a long awful day at work. Although I didn't mean to kick it hard enough to leave a mark on the wall behind, but my hands were full. I'll paint over it tomorrow and it'll be fine. I throw my bags onto the sofa, which eventually land on the floor because I didn't throw hard enough. Jasper, my ginger cat just looks at me and then the bags as if to say 'Are you going to pick that up human? A bottle of red wine waits for me in the fridge as well as my cheap packet meal. Sticking the spaghetti Bolognese in the microwave and pouring the glass for myself was all I was waiting for today. Might as well flick the television on for background noise. Where's the remote? I lift up all the cushions and look over and behind the sofas. It's gone. Meow. Oh, Jasper is sitting on it. I shoo him away, and he casually strolls into the kitchen for his dinner. The news has just started; let's see what's going on in the world. Ping! Lovely dinners ready. I'm all set now to relax and do nothing. Just as I settle on to my recliner to watch the news, all the lights in my house flicker, it goes on for a few seconds then off completely. I'm in complete darkness. Everything in my house has switched off, even the streetlights outside flicker a good few seconds. What is that smell? Burning? But everything is off in the house so it can't be in here. It must be from outside; it's a very strong smell so it must be near, so near it's set my fire alarms off. Jasper running away in terror at the loud noise. Grabbing my tea towel to wave the smoke out when suddenly...

Bang.

What was that? It sounded as if though something was thrown at the window. Wait I think there was. I slowly creep towards it, I'm a few feet away, and my lights flicker back on, startling me in the process. A note is stuck on my kitchen window.
"Run Now!"
Is this a joke? Bewildered by this message, I wasn't sure if something like this could be ignored. Screaming emerges outside in the streets. I dash to my window to get a view of what's happening. Within a few seconds I see one of my neighbours. Annie, I think her name is and her friend, what's his name again? Um. Oh, Billy that's it. They run towards the commotion. She screams "We need to get there now!" Get where? What's going on? My eyes catch the sight of a blazing orange in the distance. The thick black smoke covers the sun. My word, it looks horrendous! The farm on the other side of town is just rising up in flames, along with the church. Everyone scatters in the town centre. I look back at the note, at the writing. I recognise this writing, someone who used to be close to me. Oh no, what have you done?

KATHY'S

Knife still in hand Sally was finishing carving the chicken ready for the family's return when, without warning, the house lights went out. Within 10 seconds, before she could even reach the fuse box to investigate the cause, the lights came back on.

"Strange," she muttered to herself, but as she turned to complete her task, she saw it and gasped in shock. A note stuck to the window with the words written in large black print "RUN NOW."

"What the hell's going on? How did that note get there?" Gripping the knife closer to her, Sally slowly walked towards the window. Nothing but silence, no strange figures evident to her as she peered through the window into the evening gloom.

What should she do? Why would she need to run? Who put the note there in that short space of time? A thousand questions were running around in her head as she reached for her phone. She must call Tim. If there was a danger, he and the girls must be warned.

Before she could call the number, she heard it, first the sound of gunshot and then the screams. Terrified she dropped the phone and fell to the floor. Lying flat and still clutching the knife she inched her way towards the door, her whole body taut with fear.

Gripping the door, she pulled herself up and looked through the spy hole. Shock bit into her when she saw him. It could not be. Amir, her friend, stood there clutching the gun.

"Kill all the infidels, we will teach them they cannot attack us, "cried the tall man with the long beard. As the bullet thundered through the door, Sally fell back, blood pouring from her chest.

As Amir leaned over her, she plunged the knife into his body and mouthed the words "Why, Amir, why?"

The weight of him was heavy on her body as he clutched his stomach and fell on her. The last words she heard as the breath left her dying body were, "I did try to warn you".

BAILEY'S

"Run now!"

I grab my pre-packed emergency bag, my shoes and my pistol that I keep in my bedside table before I follow the note's instructions.

The note with the combination of lights going out tells me that it's work. It's how we communicate in cases of emergency, which means that I'm in danger. Due to my job being one a little more on the dangerous side, I always sleep in dark clothes: a black vest and leggings plus a jumper in cold seasons.

I start to run down the thousands of stairs that head away from my apartment and towards the main road (the back entrance is too time-consuming as I'd have to pick the lock). I then hide across the road behind a bush to inspect the damage that is about to be done to my now old home and as if perfectly timed two FBI trucks and one black Land Rover pulls up with men jumping out with machine guns. The woman in charge emerges from the Land Rover and shouts commands to twenty men. All this for me?

My heart begins to sink as the familiar voice reaches my slowly freezing ears. Her heels slam against the wet pavement (who wears heels to hunt someone?), and then I see her hair, which confirms my thoughts. Her blazing red hair is slightly curling, and it mirrors my own.

I fight back the tears of betrayal and run again. Thinking quickly, I begin to head in the direction of the river where I usually go to calm down. However, this journey is not a calming one. I run while pushing branches of trees out of my face as it's too dark to see the dirt path and in the small area of trees I am hidden away from the danger that's nearby. I finally reach the riverbank, and I can't help it, I place my hands over my mouth and scream, outrage taking over my body. A small boat drives up with my colleague on board.

"Thanks for the message, you saved my life" I manage to muster.

"I'm so sorry; I overheard her a few hours ago in her office. I have no idea why she did it."

I slowly climb on board a little unsure and very hesitant. I sit down, and I can't control the shivers that I feel running down my spine. I feel unnaturally weak as I look up at my good friend's stern face, the person who saved my life, yet the feeling of suspicion overrides the feeling of safety. For who can I trust when my own mother ordered my death. I stare into the water, thoughts running wild until one thought remains - 'Bye Mum'.

NATALIE'S

Her chest felt tight, as she gasped for air, staring blankly at the note. In the ten seconds, she was plunged into darkness; it felt as though her limbs had been torn apart and shoved back together like a frustrating jigsaw puzzle. Remi knew it was a risk coming home today after everything that had happened, but she needed to find the photo. The photo that proved her innocence.

'Run Now!' was scribbled on the post-it note that appeared on the window in front of her. Perhaps that's precisely what she should've done - accepted, ran and moved on. But Remi swelled with anger at the thought of being pushed out of her home again, and despite shaking vigorously from head-to-toe, she screamed towards the ceiling;

'You want me out of here?! Well come and make me!' Running frantically around the room she searched. The sofa was ripped apart; she smashed vases, tables, TVs and anything else she could lay her hands on. Only when she found the axe did she pause for breath.

The lights flickered, and everything fell silent. Remi's eyes were menacing around the room. Lights flickered once more. Her heart felt as though it was beating outside her chest. A rumbling came from under the floorboards. Gentle at first, but within a few seconds, the crashing sound beneath Remi's feet felt as though she was standing upon a tidal wave. She grabbed her ears, unable to take the noise any longer. The lights flickered. Darkness. Ten seconds later, and the lights returned. The room was silent...and empty. Only a single post-it note remained attached to a lone axe. On it, it read; 'Too Slow'.

KEV'S PROMPT

THE SHRAPNEL AT THE BOTTOM OF MY POCKET RATTLES.

ABOUT KEV

Oi, Oi, the Cockney Poet here.
I love writing short stories but prefer poetry.
I am a published poet.
My fave poet is John Cooper Clarke.
I have been a member of Pensmiths writing group for about five years.
I have written roughly 75 poems.

KEV'S

Memories flooded my mind — different times. But always memories of over there.

Nights were so black you couldn't see your hand in front of your face. Yet, the stars seem to twinkle brightly, and the sky seemed to beam like a big torch. The wind howled around our bodies and faces sounding like wolf cubs calling out to their mother.

Sgt Hawkins laid down next to me in our hole. Occasional bullets were zipping by overhead.

We were told to hanker down until the push at first light. I couldn't sleep. But the sarge went out like a light.

Sarge screamed in my ear. I must have drifted off. "Come on lad. We are moving on. As he stood up, a bullet went through one cheek and out the other. I had to act fast. I gave him morphine and looked in his mouth; the bullet had shattered his jawbone. I removed what shrapnel I could and put bandages on both cheeks. Medics came and took the sarge away.

Dozens of my fellow soldiers and I went into unknown territory. Un-leashing an obscene number of bullets. We saw bodies falling in the tree line in front of us. When we came to the trees, we all stood looking on in horror. Lying dead in front of us were what looked like boys. Boys no older than eighteen. We were told before coming out here that they use children, but it was still bloody hard seeing it. Images that will invade my mind forever.

When I got back after finishing my tour, I received a medal for saving Sgt Hawkins. I only did what anybody in that situation would have done.

I had since lost the medal. After coming back I have been forgotten about; I served my country, and my country deserted me. I have been homeless now for roughly seven months. Most of my belongings are long gone. I sleep with four other people I met on the streets. Strangely enough two were ex-paras who had also seen war.

Nights were getting colder, and even though I was used to this kind of weather, I started feeling it more in my bones. My cough was getting more severe, and with no money for medicine I had to get on with it.

This evening was so cold I swear I saw a polar bear and penguin walk pass by. I was laying down under some cardboard boxes trying to keep warm. Cold breath was leaving my mouth slower and slower. I knew I was going to die soon. I felt fragile and had trouble keeping my eyes open.

I put my hand in my pocket, and the shrapnel at the bottom rattled. It was the only thing I have kept. I sighed and slipped away, and with my dying breath, I remembered my good times over there.

JONATHAN'S

Why do I collect militaria? Despite being a pacifist, I am obsessed with the subject. Why do people go to war? Initially, I suppose it was something to do with territory or food supplies. Even if a tribe had enough land and food, it could still envy another the belongings of another tribe. Many people were wiped out due to greed; the winners wasted the spoils.

I would find it so difficult to kill someone. I suppose I would have been a conscientious objector, like my uncle, or would have surrendered if I'd had to join the armed forces, despite having flat feet. I hoped that my rivals would take pity on me. People have to be a hard-hearted person to progress from an assault to murder if they can see the face of their adversary.

Over time, people could kill from a distance using weapons such as a bow and arrow or a catapult. This meant that you couldn't see a person's face and couldn't determine body language. Isn't it human nature to be upset if you see someone looking unhappy? After all, the leaders often get others to do their dirty work.

Hiroshima was an even more significant turning point. The Japanese were the enemies. All Japanese people, no exceptions. That would be defined as racism now, but then many people considered that all the people of a nation had the same behavioural traits as their leaders. Millions were killed by the press of a button. The assailants may not have been bothered about what they were done and may have had a chat or something to drink as if nothing had happened.

The nuclear missiles are far more powerful now. Some nations can destroy the world several times over. How many times do you need to destroy Planet Earth? But the more money there is for weapons, the less there is to help solve the world's problems. How much have we really learned from George Orwell's 1984?

I think about this as the shrapnel at the bottom of my pocket rattles. I have hollowed out each piece of shrapnel and filled it with a non-volatile fluid. So far, so good. If anyone approaches me, I shall mix the contents of two pieces of shrapnel to create a nerve poison. Being a pacifist hasn't really helped me. Why should military leaders have all the fun?

MARK'S

The shrapnel at the bottom of my pocket is all I will ever have; I can't afford anything, nothing. I'm just a poor man. They say a man is rich if he has good friends, but I don't have them either.

I am and always will be alone; my only friend is the Queen on my shrapnel, must have about 84p. I'd be rich if I lived in the 90s.

What will I do with this change? Maybe it's time I changed too, stop being this way and leave. Just move on the best I can. Perhaps I'll have more than this shrapnel in my pocket? But, how do I? I'm getting old now, and a change would mean a lot. I can't do much, and I'm in pain most of the time from either my joints or a big hole inside me that has never been filled, and most likely never will. So much I want to do and see, but I lost the fight long ago. I no longer recognise myself anymore. Just a shell of what I used to be, I lost myself, I need to find that man again. The spark of life so foreign to me; but where to look?

Some find that spark at the bottom of a bottle, some find it in more colourful places. I just don't know where to find mine. I'm long past asking for help; I am alone now, just me, a long battle with my own arrogance and ego. I don't need help, I used to say, I can do it alone, but nobody can. Tears fill my eyes on a nightly basis, and I don't know why.

The shrapnel at the bottom of my pocket is what they found me with. I couldn't do it you see, I had to let go, and I lost my battle. I played many games in my life, but my life is one I couldn't win, much to my dislike, there was an easy way, and I took it, and the shrapnel? Although I can't take it with me, I left a note requesting whoever finds me, get a panda pop; they still do them, I think; it's hard to remember.

A figure appears before me and takes out a shiny 10p and asks, "Heads or tails?" I'm shocked at who this guy could be but said 'tails' anyway as a joke; it's a funny moment for me, from a tv show where the guy has a two-headed coin, and the guy calls tails. All I hear is 'you win', and with a big jolt, I'm back in my body. Is this the second chance I was after? Would my ego let me be this time? The shrapnel was gone, only notes there now. I'm surprised but not complaining; my new life awaits. Although I know I will fail again; it's happened to me so many times. Luck is just not on me, but I get up and walk away with a hope that this time there will be more than just shrapnel in my pocket. I will find myself again; Lord knows it's been a long time coming.

EMILY'S

It had been a long wait for Tom, living alone in his bungalow. He had been on a donor list for two years. Now his time had come to receive a kidney transplant. As he began to undress by the hospital bed with the curtains drawn, he heard the shrapnel at the bottom of his pockets rattle. He took out the contents, and his mind raced back twenty years to when he had narrowly survived a bomb attack. There he was ambling along, enjoying the leisure of window shopping, and going into a few stores for items on his shopping list in the mall.

Suddenly a blast was heard, followed by screams all around and people were crying. To cut a long story short, he lost one leg and shrapnel was removed from his body. He had asked the surgeon to give him some as a reminder.

Why a reminder you may wonder? Well for Tom, as devastating as the event and pain emotionally and physically was, it was a reminder from then on, how lucky he was to be alive. The shrapnel helped him along his way, as whenever he felt under the weather, or noticed himself moaning and groaning, he picked up the shards to kick start him back to a positive frame of mind.

Now, as he held the pieces of shrapnel in his hands by the hospital bed, his fear of the surgery abated. He was being given another chance to live longer, and he was so very grateful. He smiled as he put the shards in the drawer of his bedside locker. Tom then got into bed to listen to a relaxation tape before tuning in to his favourite comedians on the internet.

His operation was a success, and he was back home in his bungalow, now with a new lease of life. As for the shrapnel, oh! He still kept it.

KATHY'S

Harry couldn't understand the fuss, strangers with cameras asking him questions, staff fussing around him and all his family grinning from ear to ear. Apparently not many people reached 101, so he was something of a celebrity. He was going to be on News Night,

Sitting in the high backed chair, his hair slicked back and wearing the new navy blue suit; his mind rolled back to that Christmas morning in 1914. The war to end all wars they had called it and as Harry recalled the bitterly cold damp weather, the stench of the trenches, the constant noise of the guns from the enemy and the horror of watching his comrades lying dead and dying beside him, he knew it was true.

A thick mist enveloped him as he took the early morning watch, the thin army uniform and great coat giving him no real warmth as the cold damp air bit into him.

As the men slowly woke from their restless sleep, Jim turned to him. "What's that noise, Harry?"

Unbelievably the sound of "Oh, come all ye faithful," in German floated eerily across the stretch of ground which separated the enemies.

"Bloody hell, they're singing carols," said Bert. From the back of the trench, young Billy's beautiful welsh tenor joined in, and as they sang Christmas carols together, the young enemies stepped from their respective trenches into the narrow strip called 'No Man's Land'.

A football appeared from the German side, and within minutes the young men had formed a team and played together. For a short time on that Christmas day differences were put aside, fighting was forgotten as the young soldiers remembered better times. Cigarettes were shared, and thoughts of family and friends enjoying Xmas back home were uppermost in their minds.

But it was only a temporary truce, and as they all reluctantly returned to their trenches Harry bent and picked up the piece of stray shrapnel; a reminder to him of that brief respite in the fighting. He knew it would be harder than ever now to fire a gun at a man he had spent time so closely with — young men just like him who had no choice in what they had to do.

Harry was awoken from his reverie by a gentle nudge from his daughter. "Daydreaming again Dad?" said Sarah. "Time to blow out the candle on your cake. Only one as there's no way we could fit another 100 on," she laughed.

Harry did not know why he had been spared to live such a long and productive life while so many of his friends had suffered and died alongside him. As he put his hand in his pocket and felt the shrapnel he had placed there earlier, he thought to himself, "As long as the shrapnel in the bottom of my pocket rattles, they will never be forgotten."

BAILEY'S

"No Mum, I forgot to give Nanny a kiss!" Nine-year-old me exclaimed as I sprinted back to where my nan was laughing from the front door.

"Okay, darling. We'll wait for you in the car." My mum giggled.

I reached the doorstep and I smiled up to my nan and BOOM!

The car exploded…taking my parents with it.

The police said that the opening of the doors was the trigger. It was a murder.

Today I sit on the kerb where it happened holding the piece of shrapnel from that day. I remember the pain of watching the flames and the smell of smoke as it filled my lungs. The blood-curdling scream that emerged from behind me and the feeling of weightlessness as I'm plucked off the floor and put down safe inside. I remember the pain of a way too public funeral, the pain of a failed investigation, but today, today I feel something mixed in with the pain…relief?

Fiddling with the small piece of metal I recall the events of the last month, the roller-coaster of emotions that I went through when there was a knock at my door to tell me 'the murderer has been caught', five years later. I felt anger, sadness and relief, but mostly I'm thankful to those officers that never gave up hope.

A month ago today he was found, and now I finally know why my parent's lives had been so horribly taken and why I was also a target. It was my mother. She was the reason why. Don't get me wrong; I've forgiven her completely. Apparently, she was having an affair, but she called it quit when she became pregnant with me. He'd been plotting and debating whether to do it. He decided not to until he saw us all one day at the park, we were laughing, and he was lonely. He hated the idea of being second best, I should have been his, but I'm not so I'm a sin in his eyes.

That's what he told me a few hours ago when I looked him dead in the eye as he got sentenced to life.

I get up off the kerb and put the shrapnel into my pocket where it rattles against some coins. I walk over to my nan's house, where I now live too, and without a single word, I kiss my nan on the cheek and smile. I feel free of uncertainty as I no longer have to watch my back, I can move on now. I can make peace with my past so it can't hold me back any longer. I keep the shrapnel close to me, just like how my parents will be forever close to my heart and always in my thoughts.

VICKI'S

She was tired. She closed her milky, watery eyes and relaxed into the soft pillow. Her winter-white wispy hair blended in well with the whiteness of the pillowcase. She didn't have long left; she had known that for a while. The pitying looks that she saw on the nurse's face as they tended her were all the confirmation that she needed.

She wasn't scared. She had had a good life, and she was eager to be with her Albert again. She moved her thin arm down to her pocket in her nightdress trying to reach it, and she had a moment's panic when she couldn't feel it.

Then a warm hand took her cold one into his, and she didn't need to open her eyes to know the hand of her son Kevin, as he slipped it into her hand. She knew its shape off by heart as she had held the piece of metal in her hands many times over the past 75 years.

It was her talisman, her lucky charm, a source of comfort when she needed it. She had carried it with her everywhere that she had gone for all these years. To most, it was an ugly hunk of useless metal, but to Rose it signified hope.

During World War II, Rose had been a seventeen-year-old mother struggling to bring up her baby while her Albert was on the frontline. One day she had laid Kevin down to sleep into his pram in the front room of their small house and left the room to see about sorting dinner.

Unlike other times, the warning came too late, and there was no time to head to the bomb shelter as the planes flew overhead and dropped their loads. As one bomb dropped nearby, Rose had screamed and ran to her baby. And then another had landed right across the road, and she had feared the worse.

To this day, Rose couldn't believe the sight when she had gone into the front room. The window had been blown in, dust from the remains of her neighbour's house drifted in through the huge hole. Bricks and pieces of metal from cars that had been lining the street had taken up residence. And there amid the chaos was the pram. It had been blown across the room but had luckily remained upright and undamaged.

Kevin was in his pram screaming his head off. An inch-long piece of shrapnel lay millimetres from his head. Rose couldn't believe it. She had grabbed her baby and headed to the shelter. It was only later that she had returned to the pram to retrieve the piece of metal — her lucky charm.

It had served her well over her lifetime. And now at ninety-two, she knew it was time to let it go. She ran her fingers over the familiar edges and then placed it into her son's hand, closed his fingers over it and gently squeezed his hand. The shrapnel would be rattling in a different pocket from now on.

JONATHAN'S PROMPT

"WHO AM I IF I AM NOT MYSELF?"

ABOUT JONATHAN

"Once upon a time, I was a little boy, and my favourite school subjects were nature study and writing stories. I now have a Zoology degree and attend fiction and non-fiction writing classes. Writing stories and poems at Pen to Print helps me think quickly and develop new ideas. Fiction is not fact. It need not be logical, and you need only be limited by your imagination".

JONATHAN'S

"You're not the man I married," screamed Hazel.

Who did she expect? I was still the same man, or I thought I was. Sometimes I wasn't sure. As I moved further away from her, I wondered into her past. This wasn't as traumatic as the time I had used tachyon power to travel to another planet. I looked through a high-powered telescope and saw myself by the window, but which one was I? I couldn't be on another planet and on Earth at the same time, could I? Could my other self see me, and would I be a different age than I was then?

I could understand how Hazel felt. I hadn't been a dutiful husband, nor had I capitalised on my experiences as an astronaut. I could have been a TV star and a successful author, but I wasn't. My therapist said, "The world is full of could haves, but I need you to say what you have achieved. Even if you believe in reincarnation, you probably only have one shot at life. Only one of your father's sperms successfully fertilised one of your mother's eggs. If it had been another sperm, you would be a different person. You should be grateful for that one-in-a-billion chance."

I wondered if my therapist really understood me. Surely, I was more than a fertilised egg, but was my life pre-recorded or did my choices in life lead to my current feelings of unhappiness?

I usually spent my nights turning around in my bed, being awoken by Hazel hitting me in my ribs to stop me snoring or complaining that she was cold if I took too much of the duvet. I sometimes wondered if it would be better if we slept apart, but would that lead to the end of our marriage? I couldn't really cope being by myself, even if I had a multiple personality.

One night, I left my body and watched myself and Hazel lying in our bed. Hazel seemed quite peaceful, and I wasn't snoring, assuming I was in the bed and not the entity connected by a golden cord to my still body. I wondered what would happen if Hazel had suddenly woken and how she would have reacted. Was my body colder than before? Would she think I was dead? Who could she phone at this time of night?

I could only assume that I would return to my body before dawn. Did I want to? It was relatively peaceful up here, and I glimpsed a tunnel with a glowing light at the end. This was supposed to be a relatively common experience. If I stretched the golden cord to breaking point, I could travel to an idyllic place and be with people who cared for me, but would this be me and would the dead body below be me as well?

I still cared for Hazel, and I wondered if she still cared for me. My therapist had told me that the people who cared most for me were those who got angry with me. The people who were not concerned showed no real interest, one way or another. There was no point in them risking my wrath if they didn't want me to feel better about myself.

Should I break the golden cord?

MARK'S

What am I if I'm not myself? A shell of a man dead inside with nowhere to hide; like an ex-con who agrees to one last ride.

Who am I if I'm not myself? The man in the mirror looking back I don't know; least I think I'm a man, I can't tell I've lost my glow.

What am I if I'm not myself? Do you know? Answers on a postcard please, I'll send a stamp; my own family call me a tramp.

Who am I if I'm not myself? Where did all the pictures go from the shelf? Small children there used to be; now there's just me.

Who am I if I'm not myself? I don't know. When did all these big trees grow, and the apples that fall from a tree, so tall?

Who am I if I'm not myself? I'm sick of that question now, or maybe I'm just sick? Another victim of the dreaded cancer click.

Who was I when I was myself? When the pictures were on the shelf, when I could look and see a man I recognised, not this shell all broken by lies. Who was I when I was myself? What would them postcards read? Would the one true, I'll stick to it like glue, if only I could find myself.

Who was I? Don't matter, only who I am now; the old me is dead, long live the king. I worry too much over such a little thing.

Who I was I hated, and who I am I now love, this new me fits perfect like a glove.

So who am I if I'm not myself? Well, that's easy, you see, for after much soul-searching I find that the answer is; I am me.

Not the one before; but a me whose future looks bright, and one who will stand tall and ready for a fight. For a time must come in every man's life when he must ask...Who am I if I'm not myself?

EMILY'S

Oh well, just write whatever comes to mind, as she put pen to paper and gradually one sentence flowed after another.

Jane chose the title "Who am I if not myself." As it was a City and Guilds course, it had to encompass young children and education. So, her title was "Myself" and her story is as follows.

As a child, I was relatively quiet; in fact, very shy, and I actually dreaded being chosen to read out loud. Why? Well, it meant standing up, having all eyes on me. The teacher I dreaded the most as negative criticism instead of positive feedback was her way of commenting.

When all this started, I really cannot say as it seemed to be all my school life. The reader may wonder what type of schools this bright woman attended. My positive feedback is that I went to Catholic schools run by nuns. I can assure you if I had my time over again, I would steer clear of specific nuns in those schools.

Actually, my Primary Headteacher was alright. Then I feel a bitterness that worsens as I recall Junior and Secondary Headteachers. These two people obviously did the best they could, which was for sure not good enough for me.

It seemed to me that they misused their power as teachers and worse still as nuns. Were those my feelings then or now? Well, it seems both. I also know it was a combination of an unhappy home life at times. The result being I was not happy at home or at school.

The bizarre situation was that at sixteen years of age, I left school without qualifications. Then throughout adulthood, I found myself back in learning environments. At times I would think "What am I doing here? Why am I putting myself through this again?"

The answer is I am making up for the lost time, albeit it slowly, while laying to rest negative experiences of the past, which almost ruined the potential of the child inside me.

I like every other child had the potential; then it was systematically chipped away throughout my childhood. Maybe that is why I am here on this particular course. I really know what it feels like to be anxious, shy and want positive feedback, not negative criticism. I will remember that when faced with children — especially the quiet ones in a nursery or school environment.

Kindness does not cost anything as my Mother used to say.

Well, it was difficult to begin my essay as I wanted to be honest in giving a real picture of my early memories of education.

Well shucks, I only went and did it, and oh my goodness it brought up painful memories of my school life. However, it felt cathartic.

Who am I if not myself? Nowadays, with knowledge of mindfulness, I am discerning with people, whether family, friends, acquaintances or those I meet along my way. I am assertive speaking my mind. Remembering my Mother's words "Kindness does not cost anything."

SKY'S

The school bell rings at three o'clock, and the children rush out of the classrooms to freedom.

Chris looks at the big red F on his mathematic test; Jason jumps on his back, messing up Chris's hair.

"What's with the long face?" Jason has been Chris's best friend since they were in primary school; they know everything about each other.

"There's only so much failure I can take from my subjects."

"Oh come on, who cares? Don't worry when we leave school, we'll still own companies and be rich!" Chris always enjoyed Jason's enthusiasm.

"Anyway, I've got something to show you," Jason grabs Chris and guides him out of the fire exit of the school.

"Apparently the buildings been abandoned for a while now, lots of weird stuff happened here." Chris is just hoping Jason's curiosity doesn't get them in trouble.

Jason draws the curtains, and there stands a door-sized gold mirror, the diamonds glitter in the sunlight, illuminating the room.

"Here it is!" Jason's voice shrieked with excitement.

"Seriously? You brought us here to look at a mirror that I could have bought in shopping centre?" Jason ignored that question, for he knew he was in for a surprise.

"How did you know something like this was even here?" Chris asked.

"My dad worked on the building, remember? There were rumours about it. Apparently, it made some

blokes go mad at each other and fights broke out"
Chris did not like the sound of this.

"Here stand in front of it and see if it works." Chris looks into the mirror; he only sees himself staring back.

"This was a waste of time." Jason grabs Chris's arm.

"Just wait!"

Chris turns to look back at himself, within moments a thick black cloud smears the reflection. He sees himself standing in front of a large audience, belting out every joke he can, the crowd love him. They have tears of laughter. Chris removes the mask he is wearing, which is strange since he was unaware that he was wearing one. All he sees now are tears, but the tears are not water, its black liquid that falls down his cheeks. The crowd see this, and soon their laughter disappears. They slowly move away from him. He now stands there. Alone. Nothing but darkness surrounds him now, his heart rate increases; he finds it hard to breathe. Why won't this stop? Jason shakes Chris.

"What the hell is the matter with you?" Jason grabs Chris and pulls him back.

"You didn't see it?"

"No, I only your reflection."

Chris is shaken from what he saw, is that who he really is? Does this mirror tell the future? Or show you who you are? He takes a step back and leans by the wall trying his best to gather his thoughts. Jason takes his turn in front of the mirror. A green mist clouds his reflection; he stands in a suit, leaning on the window in a high-class tower looking over London. All there is outside his window is poverty. Destruction. With stacks of money on his desk, he has no worries.

"Wow, not to brag but the future seems to be looking up for me."

Chris listens to his friend. What did he see in there?

"Soon, I'll be rich; powerful even." Chris stares at him. Who is he? Who am I?

KATHY'S

Who am I if I am not myself?
Am I a lonely parcel placed on a shelf?
Am I an alien flown in from mars,
to mix with the earthlings who eat things in jars?
Am I a naughty cat who prowls around the garden?
Catching the mice, scratching the sofa and spilling the rice.
Or perhaps I'm a frog who croaks in the dark,
and scares all the people who walk in the park.
I could be an actor who plays many parts, somebody different every month of the year, laughing and crying without any fear.
But at the end of the day, I'm happy being myself,
because I don't think I'd look that good as a little green elf.

BAILEY'S

Who am I if I'm not myself?
Difficult question.
Complex answer.
To work out the answer, I need to know who the real me is.
Me
When I'm with my friends
I'm happy, carefree.
A little self-conscious,
With a need to fit in and conform.
No, that's not me.
Me.
The family girl.
Oh, so caring and a heart full of gold.
I feel accepted, protected
And as if I'm under a blanket of love.
That me hits closer to home.
Me
The student, the worker.
I always put my work first,
Head down and study hard.
Full of stress and anxiety, unsure when to let my hair down.
That's not me. No.
Me.
I am the girl with her head in a book.
A paintbrush in my hand.
Dancing around until I feel exhausted.
The shy girl who hides behind a wall of confidence.
The daughter of an author who's my biggest inspiration.
The daughter of a protective dad who does nothing but
love me.
The sister of two brothers who are the loves of my life.
I listen before jumping to conclusions.
I understand before I try to help.
I love.
I love bands and music.

I love movies,
People and animals.
But I also hate,
I'm only human.
But I'm not all perfect, and I know that.
That's what makes me
Me.
Who am I if I'm not myself?
It's easy to answer now.
I'm the obedient student,
I'm the quick-tempered,
The girl surrounded by friends.
The quiet one of the class.
Those aren't me.
They are only part of me.
They don't define me.
Therefore, they are not *me*.

VICKI'S

Everybody has different roles to play,
Along the journey of their life.
They start the second a first breath is taken,
And range from being a daughter to a wife.
So, which of these roles define a person?
Or do they serve to trap you in?
When I look at myself in the mirror,
Am I trapped within my own skin?

My role as a daughter at first was easy,
I had a loving and safe childhood.
My teenage years, and a few after that,
I was blessed, and all was good.
Then disaster struck, and our roles were reversed,
And I did the best that I could.

Now I'm a daughter to one; a heart broke in two,
Still a child, despite being in womanhood.

My role as a mum has been challenging,
But my kids mean the world to me,
Each of them holds a place in my heart,
And I'm proud of who they have turned out to be.
Mason is now grown and independent,
Bailey is a smaller version of me,
Ethan is definitely his own person,
And, there's my unborn, I love them, all three.

My role as a wife is ever-changing,
As is the love that I have for him.
At first, things were all of a flutter,
When I didn't see him, life felt so grim.
When the children were small, life changed,
The days just all seemed to blend,
However, we are now older and wiser,
And my husband completes me; my best friend.

I'm also a sister, aunt and friend,
These roles are important to me.
Now we are grown being a sister is easy,
Our parent's children stand together, all three.
I'm an aunt to several nieces and nephews,
And I'm very proud of them all,
And although my pool of friends is tiny,
I know we have each other when we fall.

In my later years, another role has developed,
The writer in me has burst out.
This role has been slowly simmering away,
Until one day it burst out to shout,
"Hey girl, you have always dreamed,

Of seeing your words in print,
It won't happen unless you give it a go!"
Now I'm alive! My eyes have a glint!

Another role has been forced upon me,
It's a role that I wish would sod off.
I've become a prisoner within my own body,
I wish all that I had were a cough!
Chronic illnesses course through and consume me,
I've become an invalid; A burden; A weight.
My life now revolves around health issues,
And I've put so much on my family's plate!

Now, Who Am I? Am I not myself?
Which of all those roles, if any, define me?
Take the best of these roles, and the worst,
They combine, that's the person you see.
But that's just a version; it's not real,
The real me I keep hidden inside,
My husband and kids, they know me,
As to everyone else, well, I'll continue to hide.

KEV'S

I awoke at dawn, cold from the night chill. The sun appeared over the top of the Rocky Mountains. Dying embers of my fire gave me a warmish coffee. I washed my face in the nearby shallow creek and pogoed up onto my horse.

For two long days, I have been searching for Crazy Kez, the most dangerous gunslinger in the west. He had robbed four banks and killed innocent people so far, and because of his mask, nobody knew what he looked like.

I rode on towards Tombstone; I needed some proper rest.

I was riding out of town fast, and I didn't know why, or how long I had even been in Tombstone. This had happened several times before where I came upon town and hey bingo, I'm leaving fast. My mind was wandering; I couldn't remember much lately, only that I was Sheriff Mack Arshall and was after Crazy Kez.

Later that day, I came upon a cave; I got off my horse and entered the cave. I looked around and found several chests full of money. There were unused wicker lights stuck to the walls and more around a massive unlit fire. I lit the fire and a couple of the lights, the whole cave flickering in shadows. In the far corner laying on the stony ground were two skeletons. I had no idea who they were.

Six chests were completely loaded to the top with money, who brought these here and who are the bodies? I had a deep feeling that I had been here before; something seemed vaguely familiar. On the left wall were some drawings, they showed three men, one wearing a mask that looked like it was made of skin.

I walked back out and gathered my stuff together and went back into the cave. I rifled through my stuff and found some banknotes loose in the bottom of one of my sacks. How did these get in there? I continued going through my sacks and what I found next floored me.

A voice shouted from outside. "Crazy Kez, you are surrounded, come out with your hands up."

My whole demeanor changed; I put on the mask I had found in my sack. I was now Crazy Kez. I felt strong and aggressive, and I wanted blood. I put out the fire and lights and stood in complete darkness waiting. Shots rang out, hitting the walls around me. I fired back and heard groans as my bullets hit flesh.

Out of the blue, a single bullet hit my left leg and splintered the bone. My bandana made a good tourniquet to help stem the blood.

Hours had gone by with no more shots fired or any communication. Then I heard what appeared to be more horses arriving. I had a bad feeling my time was up. But I wasn't giving up without a fight, after all, I am Crazy Kez.

During the quiet moments, I had remembered who the two skeletons were. It was Humpy Harry and One-eyed Jim: my comrades in arms. I had brought them back here after previous jobs went wrong.

More shots suddenly ricocheted off the cave walls.

"We are coming in, in ten minutes, come out now and surrender" a voice came out. "I am Sheriff Mack Arshall" the voice continued

I stood stock-still; my mind is whirling with a thousand thoughts a minute.

"Who am I if not myself?" I thought as a hundred bullets drilled into my body.

MARK'S PROMPT

I'M SITTING HERE ON THE EDGE OF THE WORLD THINKING ABOUT LIFE.

ABOUT MARK

I'm one of the original members of the group, and I have to say that I am very thankful for being a part of it. Over the years, not only has being a member increased my confidence, but my writing has improved, and my imagination freed. I have made some good life-long friends.

MARK'S

They're all six feet under. It's done. The pogo killer has killed her last family member; avenged! And now I'm sitting on the edge of the world thinking about my life. The new life that awaited me down there in the city that's so peaceful at night, hiding the sin behind a dark blanket. All I see in the dark are the faces of the men that I have killed and a thought -did I do the right thing? Did all the monsters I killed in their name make me one too? And would I have a line of people waiting to find me for the same reason I hunted them? Who knew? All I knew is that in a few minutes they might get their wish.

Jenny has suspected me since that case we undertook at the house. She said that I knew my way around the house too well; from then on I knew that I was being watched and I was taken off the case for hunting for the pogo killer, because of lack of results they said. I agreed and let them get on with it. I already knew who was next and took them out quick. They're searching for clues across the street to me, searching for phantom clues that I know are not there. The new life I wanted I could no longer have as if I left now it would be too fishy, so I made the call to dispatch that I was chasing the killer on the roof. That's when Jenny arrived all 'Gung Ho', so I shot her in both kneecaps and picked up her gun and shot myself in the shoulder. I had a smoke while she bled out, then I passed out from blood loss.

I awoke two days later in a nearby hospital, and I hear how they found the evidence I planted and about how Jenny was the killer. Apparently, she was unstable and had died from my shots. I explain how I hadn't wanted that but took one in the shoulder and passed out; they ate it up, believed it all, as I hoped.

When I got out, I quit the force for personal reasons, Jenny was my friend, and I killed her. Just an excuse, I killed loads of men, all with a pogo stick. I got my new life. I visit Jenny from time to time to say sorry, it helps you know.

So, if you find this letter, this is my confession, that I, Detective Kate Malone, is the pogo killer, not Detective Jenny Forrest.

EMILY'S

Edward was in a world of his own. He had stayed at home for the past fortnight, not going out or talking to anyone. In fact, though he had a house phone and internet connection, he had unplugged both many weeks before.

Why may you wonder?

Well, during the past two years while grieving for his loved one, he had gradually pulled away from life outside. Declining invitations, stopping his leisure activities golf, painting and amateur dramatics. He had been retired four years ago and now had scant motivation.

He felt disconnected, having no enthusiasm for anything or anyone.

As Edward sat by his front room window looking out at the sky, trees and his garden, he said out loud to no one but himself. "I'm sitting here on the edge of the world thinking about life." A few minutes later he added, " shall I bother, can I, is it worth it, now in my senior years as I feel tired of trying. It seems so so hard on my own."

Ruminating over past memories; happy, sad, traumatic, uplifting; oh, so many flooded his mind.

All of a sudden, he saw a robin fly to the bird stand. Edward felt a tug of guilt as he had not replenished it with birdseed and fresh water for over a week. It was a must-do job for him thrice weekly usually. He stood up slowly and went to the kitchen, opening the pet cupboard to see a small opened bag of birdseed. He took that along with a bottle of water and sauntered out to the garden to feed the birds. He began humming the song "Feed the birds" from the film Mary Poppins, then quietly singing it. On his return indoors he heard Kitty his cat of seven years meowing at the window to come in.

Well, that was his 'aha' moment. He opened the window holding out his arms to her. She nudged his hand and purred as with tears in his eyes; he lifted her up to give her a heartfelt hug. Kitty had been missing for three days, and he had given up hope of seeing her again.

He gave her fresh food and water, noting that along with no birdseed left, there was only one tin of cat food. He looked out at the garden spotting two robins now at the bird stand along with a chaffinch and two sparrows busily eating the seeds.

He slowly walked upstairs to get showered and dressed. The warm water felt uplifting as it was his first in many weeks.

As he dressed, he chatted to himself out loud, saying "I can do this, it is worth it. I'm done with sitting on the edge of the world thinking about life — my own pity party. I've missed feeding the birds and squirrels. I missed little Kitty so so much. Maybe she fled for a while as pissed off with my melancholy."

As he went downstairs opening the front door, he muttered "That's it, one step at a time," locking the door behind him.

He sauntered up the road to the supermarket to stock his cupboards with food for himself, Kitty, birds and squirrels.

On returning home, he plugged in the phone and internet, when charged up he took a few slow deep breaths as he dialled his pal Doug's number.

"Hi mate," said Doug, "Where have you been? I haven't seen you for months. I did ring a few times."

"Oh, long story Doug, I'll tell you when we meet up. I'm here now. Do you fancy a game of golf next week?"

Doug said, "Ooh, yes, that sounds like a good plan." So, the two pals met as arranged, had a game of golf and a heart to heart buddy chat.

Edward was slowly getting his life back on track. He was determined to move, well away from the edge of the world, while thinking about life. He was now reconnecting, albeit it slowly with people and leisure activities. It felt good, and he was proud of himself.

Edward smiled as he remembered the robin on the empty bird stand. That was the kick up the backside he needed to wake him from sadness in order to reconnect with life and truly live not just exist.

SKY'S

My god, the view really is mesmerising. I allowed my legs to collapse just to the edge of the cliff, letting them dangle. In the distance the sun was setting behind the large hotels, the bright lights of Las Vegas begin to illuminate the sky. I'm still slightly drunk from drinking most of the day, pretty sure drugs were used at some point as well, but not that bad that I can't admire the view.

Wow, I didn't realise how far I've travelled. Further, then I wanted. The last thing I remember was gambling in Bellagio, basically throwing my money away at poker. I could feel my pockets burning from the money I was losing so thought I should call it quits. I needed some air anyway, so I stumbled away from my competitors and took a stroll, accidentally knocking into people. To be fair, they looked off their heads as well, so I doubt they'll remember me, though this one in particular did.

"Watch it!" my body was shoved to the side. This guy had some nerve.

"Piss off, you muppet!" Probably shouldn't have said that. This guy was twice my size, what was I thinking? Why didn't I just walk away?

THUMP!

A car horn startles me; my head was resting on the curb while my body lay in the road. Wait, was I asleep?

"You okay sir?" A small man wearing a clown outfit stands over me.

Oww! My nose was bleeding, plus my head was thumping like the inside of a drum. "Yeah, just take me to the desert will ya mate."

"You sure sir?" he was slightly confused at this request.

"Yes."

Hold on, why did I want to go to the desert? There's nothing there but sand.

He opens the passenger door for me, I try my best to get myself up into the car, so he didn't have to, but my body just wouldn't co-operate.

"Allow me." He grabs hold of me and lumbers me over his shoulder. For a small man he was incredibly strong. He throws me in the cab and my head slams on the leather seat. That could have knocked me out itself. Closing the door, he walks around the cab, his shoes make a horn noise with every step.

What was this music he was playing? Why would they play this on any radio? This could easily put me in a trance if I let it.

"Just relax sir; it'll all be over soon."

What did he just say? What will be over? Using the little strength, I had to sit upright, everything I saw is something I'll never forget. The hotel lights detach themselves from the buildings and twirl around the cab, like looking inside a kaleidoscope. Looking from the window every pedestrian's faces were all animals. Unless they were masks, if they were, they deserve an award. The traffic lights scream as they stare at me with glowing eyes. The screeches pierce my ears. The cab driver laughing his head off at god knows what. My hands grab each side of my head; what the hell is going on? JUST STOP! STOP IT NOW!

BANG!

Oww, I'm in even more pain now. My eyes shot open, heart pounding in my chest. What the fuck just happened?! I'm covered in sand or should I say buried in it. It takes a few minutes for me to get my bearings until I realise where I eventually ended up.

And that's how I got here. Feet dangling over the edge of a cliff, thinking about life. The sweat drips down the side of my face, I reach for my tissue to wipe it, but instead all I got was a pocket full of sand. Great! My tuxedos ruined. That's fine. I'll just buy a new one.

I mean it's not like I can't afford it right?

I only got here because of my father.

"All right everyone, listen up! I have big news!" My dad bellowed to the office. People swivelled in their seats to face him.

"Your pregnant sir?" The office erupted into laughter.

"Ha-ha yes, and you're the father, Ricky!" The laughter continued. "No no, my son, Romeo will now be CEO of the company!"

The look on my colleague's faces said it all. Shock, disbelief and confusion all in one. If anything, I felt the same as them. I haven't actually done anything outstanding in order for me to get a promotion, but I still work my arse off none the less. We'd all be celebrating by a weekend in Las Vegas. I had no idea he planned on promoting me, so I was just as surprised as everyone else. I raised my glass of champagne with everyone else, but the atmosphere felt so frosty. This should have been a great moment for me; instead it was the worst I've had so far. I could hear them all sneering as the afternoon went on, making comments "just because I'm his son, of course, I'm gonna get all the promotions". I understand their reasons, but it's not my fault. I didn't ask for it, but that doesn't mean I can't be grateful about it. Everyone soon dispersed, and I was left standing with my father. Two colleagues congratulated me which was very thoughtful of them. Everyone else? Well. We didn't really have much to say.

The champagne bottle hangs in my pocket, dragging. Empty of course, as I try getting the last trickle from the bottom of the bottle. This should be a weekend of a lifetime, of celebration. Instead, it's just a weekend of grief. I only question is it worth it? Is this really what I want?

KATHY'S

I'm sitting here on the edge of the world staring into space and wondering where lies Mars, and all those other planets beyond the twinkling stars.
As I look down upon the Earth, I marvel at what I see, The beauty of the planet, the vastness of the seas.
The rainforests that give us life and help us all to breathe, waterfalls and mountains, snow and ice and sun, the beauty of the planet, there for everyone.
Huge crops of fruits and vegetables, rice and cocoa beans, coffee, tea and other delicate plants growing on fertile lands, picked for all of us to eat by gentle caring hands.
Animals of every shape and size, from polar bears to tigers, elephants and bears, camels on the shifting desert sand, all jostling for their place on this enormous land.
But as I sit and contemplate, I feel a sense of despair when I think of all the wars, people fighting with each other, poverty and homelessness, and anger everywhere.

They are chopping down the rainforests and killing all the creatures in the sea with plastics that will not rot for centuries to come, and I wonder if we will still survive in this place we now call home.

If the people do not heed the warning of global warming, then I dread to think what this world will become.

I wonder, is there life on other planets, and if they ever visit us what would they say, would they shake their heads in sorrow and look on in dismay?

But then I feel a glimmer of hope that maybe we still have time to change.

I like to think we could reverse the damage that's been done, that there is still hope for us to learn from our mistakes, to appreciate and enjoy this wonderful world for everybody's sake.

BAILEY'S

I sit staring out at the scenic view before me just thinking about the last few years of my life. I remember the rush of excitement I felt when I finally found it. Earth. The planet most gossiped about due to the thousands of different forms of alien that roam it. My interest in learning about these forms of life is what had led me there. I landed my ship, and that's when all my hopes were shattered. They had deadly weapons pointed straight at me from the moment I opened my doors to them. The humans yelled in a language I do not understand completely, but I have tried learning. I know enough of it to understand that they didn't want me there. Humans are the most fascinating creatures;

they only have two legs and one heart. They're pretty easy to kill thinking about it.

Earth was not what I expected. The grass wasn't as green, and the inhabitants weren't welcoming, the air was contaminated. I was taken to an isolated location where I spent two years of my life. I will never get that part of my life back. As I begin to recall, those year's I roll up the long sleeves on my arm to help the memories flood back. I close my eyes, and I remember the cage and the feeling of my blood leaving my body with each test or experiment. Do I heal when they cut there? What happens if they don't feed me? I'm still a life form, but they fail to see beyond our differences. In fact, they fail to see the similarities between themselves.

Again, I look at my arms, the scar's they have given to me. My green skin tattooed by pain. I look back out to the view ahead of me. It took me a year and a half to get here from Earth. I managed to escape after I finally managed to gather enough strength to disintegrate the brick wall that confined me to the dirtiest room ever to exist. I found my ship (they were trying to fly it, but they don't have enough legs) and I flew as far as I could. That's how I ended up here, The Edge Of The World. It's much better here. Safer. The planet is full of rental apartments perfectly designed for relaxation; they have whatever you need, no matter your species. Everything is clean and fresh, and they have a fantastic healthcare system that cared for my wounds that I was unable to tend to due to my lack of medical knowledge.

Before me, the sun begins to rise, and my last day on this planet has come. I'm leaving tomorrow. I can't let what's happened to me hold me back from future discoveries. Plus, I need to promote the book I have written, 'The Warnings of Planet Earth'. I wrote it while I was here healing, waiting for my internal wounds to heal as well as the physical ones. Life is worth living, and you can be better than your past. Your intentions and your mind are what defines you, never let your bad times hold you back. Life is what you make it. It's not all good but make sure to care for yourself, mentally and physically. Sitting here has helped me discover this knowledge. I won't let the marks on my skin stop me as they're not flaws.

The sun rising dragged my thoughts back to the now. I stand up and walk back to my house, feeling empowered to do anything.

VICKI'S

I'm sitting here on the edge of the world thinking about life. This was our place, but today I am here alone. The picnic blanket looks big without you sitting next to me. The three hours walk to get here had been lonely. But the journey had to be made; you had made that clear before you left me; the letter was only to be opened at 'our place'.

I'd considered cheating and opening it at home; after all, there was no way that you would ever know where I was when I read it. It was only a fleeting thought. You knew I would want to come here to our place, one last time. This was the only place in the world that I could properly say goodbye.

I edged myself forward so that my legs dangled over the edge of the mountainside. You would never sit like this, too scared of the height, but you really loved the view.

Why did you have to leave?

This place felt different without you. Even the walk that I usually love felt wrong. We walked through it all to get here; rough lanes, riverside paths, across two old disused railway bridges, up and down rocky slopes and around a lake.

We knew all the routes that covered this area, all the paths and bridleways. We walked the ancient lanes together that connected old farms and their out-lying hamlets.

We had sat at the edge of the waterfall delighting in the light spray that hit us.

These places were visited by lots of other travellers, so over time we explored further, we pushed ourselves and walked the rollercoaster edge of a rocky summit that was laid out with no logic at all.

Then one day we found it. Here. Our place. On the edge of the world.

The place is full of memories. It was here that we declared our love, where I asked you to move in with me. We decided the time was right to start a family here.

I hold your letter in my hand; I hesitate to open it. Once I do, that will be it. You will be gone, and I will never be able to get that moment back again, but I have to do it, I have to read your words.

Dear Katie,

I wish with all my heart that I was there with you now. You are my life, my world. I hope that you understand why I have left you. Please don't try to find me; it will just be a waste of your time.

I can't bear the idea of you watching me die. I can't bear to see the pain I'd be causing you etched into your beautiful face. I don't want to see you crying because of me. The time that I have left, I don't want to spend in a hospital bed, hooked up to a machine. I don't want you looking after me like that. You are the love of my life, not my nurse.

Not having treatment was a hard decision to make, a few months will now be a few weeks, but the harder decision was leaving you. So, remember me while you sit there, at our place. Take a deep breath and be brave. Things will get better.

Please don't grieve for me for too long. I want you to meet someone else and have those children that we were so desperate for.

Cry but laugh. Mourn but live.

Just come here now and then and remember me, I will live forever through you.

Love you forever, Mark x

My hands shake, and tears are streaming down my face. I take a deep breath and take it all in. I look at the rolling hills, ploughed fields and different types of trees and the ruins in the distance of once used farmhouses. I hear the different bird songs, the insects making their various calls, and the wind blowing around my head and through the branches of the trees. I feel the wet dew of the grass under my fingers, the sun hitting my face, and the wind whipping my hair. The sun is just breaking through the clouds; the view is truly spectacular. Spectacular, but bleak and lonely.

I take another deep breath. You brought me to this place to say goodbye, for me to see that the world carried on without you, as must I, but you are wrong. You are my world, and without you, my life does not go on.

I shuffle myself closer to the edge, close my eyes and jump.

KEV'S

I'm sitting here on the edge of the world thinking about life. About my life and the turn it took ten years ago.

It was a cold December, in the run-up to Christmas, England was in a mess. Youths were running riot, stealing anything that was not tied down and stabbing any innocent person. My wife and daughter had gone out to the local shopping centre, at about one o'clock, all hell broke out. Thousands of teens ran amok in Romford, they attacked anybody in their way and fought amongst each other.

From the killing of my family to the time the police came and told me nobody was arrested for their murder; I was wandering around like a zombie. For several months I didn't see anybody, and I decided to move out of Dagenham.

All the anger and despair I put into my new career; I didn't make friends because they came with too much baggage.

First time I felt alive again came one night in June, after a lovely warm day with families laughing and enjoying life. A fight broke out, the drunken man shouted and abused mothers with shocked children looking on. I don't know why I did what I did, but I followed him out of the park and down the street. When I was sure it was quiet enough, I picked up a brick from a garden and struck him on the head. He went down like a sack of shit. I hit him more and more, and when I was sure he had stopped breathing, I arose and walked away slowly.

After that evening, I went out more, looking for troublemakers, trying to make a difference, but not really making a dent. But I didn't actually care; I was enjoying punishing these worthless twats. My weapons got more macabre; I had a wooden baseball bat with nails hanging out. And a large pickaxe handle with three hammers attached.

My favourite was a staple gun that I adapted to shoot out tacks; this was a killer; the tacks flew into the skin of the little scroats I hunted.

For nine months, I did this, and the police knew but didn't have time to do anything about me. They had limited resources trying to keep the streets safe. But they were floundering and losing.

Newsflashes from around the world were frightening; adults killing adults; kids killing kids; the human race had gone mad.

I put my new plan into play, tackling small crime didn't concern me anymore; I had to go big to make a difference. I used my knowledge of the chemicals that I had learnt from in my new job.

I am sitting here on the summit of Mount Everest. Three months later, I released the deadly gas into the air from up here, knowing what it will do to humankind. But it had to be done.

The radio went quiet roughly a month ago, and the last report was about millions of people dying. I know I have committed Genocide, but the world needed it, we were a rotten lot of so-called humans, I hope mother nature strives.

JONATHAN'S

I'm sitting here on the edge of the world
Thinking about my life
Why am I here with nobody to care?
I have never had a wife.
What mistakes did I make?
Why did my parents die?
Was it something I said? Was I too young to know?
But not too old to cry?
I was left on my own with my negative thoughts
And no way to tie loose ends.
I feel all alone and as sad as can be
Why do I have no true friends?
As the world spins around, I look down far below
And am watched from up above
There is something out there that has shown how to care
And is showering me with love.
What could this thing be? Can it bring sanctity?
Or will I stay upon the shelf?
"Before you are loved, you must look at your soul
And appreciate yourself."
How can I love my weaknesses?
How can I bear my pain?
The shower passes me by as I'm starting to cry
And I'm in the pits again.
"What happened to Matilda?
"What about Janie May?
"They said that they cared, and you soon disappeared
"As they made you run away."
"What about the sterling work you did?
"What about your career plan?"
I wasted my wealth on an obvious scam
And it all went down the pan.

I got the sack, and I never went back.
My landlord kicked me out.
I lived in a box by a popular shop
And began to scream and shout
This wasn't me, but what could I do?
My life had come undone
So, I'm now sitting here on the edge of the world
With a new life just begun.
How can I live life differently?
Could my life be a success?
I wallow away, alone every day
Must my life still be a mess?
Will the spirit out there show me how to care?
Can I enjoy my life again?
Can I still win in a life without sin?
Will my heart work with my brain?

EMILY'S PROMPT

CHARACTER: UNSETTLED ANNIE
SETTING: AT HOME IN A NOISY TOWN CENTRE   WORDS: WHAT A NIGHT TO REMEMBER

ABOUT EMILY

I write because it's relaxing and takes me away from personal agenda along my way, albeit for a short while. It's wonderful to create characters and scenarios of my own choosing.
I am in a writer's group for two years now and so enjoy meeting up with others.
It's so interesting hearing other people's versions from our long-term story titles, plus our weekly ten-minute prompt stories.

Some members have since left, and I appreciate their contribution.

EMILY'S

It was a bitterly cold night in December. The main road was it's usual for a Saturday at midnight. Noise from the volume and beat of music bellowing out from two nightclubs five minutes apart in the distance. As for the revellers, well groups of people would go in and out, and as the night progressed, voices would get louder. Already Annie had heard three police vans; sirens on, go past. Was it trouble in the clubs? She didn't know as did not go to the window to look. It was freezing indoors as the heating had stopped working. So, there she was clad in extra layers, a hat, mittens and water bottles for her feet and lap as she watched television.

About 1 am, tired and looking forward to a good night's sleep; she goes to bed. A while later getting up to go to the bathroom, from feeling peaceful, she was now uneasy after shrieking before returning to her bed. Annie told her daughter late the next morning about the incident; who miraculously had not been woken by the shrieks. Delia giggled while listening to her Mum. Weeks later, Annie smiled about that night. Within months she not only smiled when Delia would relate the tale; she would giggle as she could see the funny side.

Hold on a minute reader as I know you are wondering what made Annie shriek when she visited the bathroom in the wee small hours of that morning. Well, here's the reason. While half asleep and sitting on the toilet, a mouse ran past her legs. Yes! It was a shock. Can you envisage it? In the next moment, she had jumped up onto the toilet seat in a panic. As for the mouse, who was probably just as startled, it scarpered under the gap at the bottom of the door. A few minutes went by before Annie stepped off the toilet; opening the door and peering around and with no sight of the mouse, she went back to bed a wee bit shaken. She wondered where had the mouse come from and where had it now gone? Oh well, she thought, I will check out the whole place tomorrow, it's disappeared for now. On her next bathroom visit, again sleepy but needs must with toilet, all of a sudden there it frigging was again — a mouse, sitting in the corner. The same mouse or his friend come to visit, Annie didn't know?

What was her reaction? Well, what would yours be? Wait for it folks; she let out a shriek and quick as a flash it ran past her legs and out under the door. She was standing on top of the toilet yet again. It was an action replay. She wondered if it had returned to go down the same hole it had come from. On inspection of the bathroom, she saw a small hole in the floorboard by the window. She was about to plug it up with toilet paper and thought; No! That is where the mouse wants to return to reach home. Reluctantly, she left it knowing that in a few hours she would be up for the day ahead. Hoping it would go down there soon and its little mousey friends don't come up to join him before she got to plug it up for good.

So, Annie still somewhat uneasy crawled back into bed. There we are reader, Annie's shrieks explained.

Now, when thinking of her daughter's comment, "Oh Mum, it's only a little mouse, it wouldn't hurt you. It was more frightened of the size of you towering over it."

Annie can now giggle. However, she wouldn't like a repeat performance.

Oh, what a night to remember.

SKY'S

"How are you holding up Annie?" Billy places his hand on her shoulder as Annie sits with her head in her lap. A bandage is wrapped around her head, and she is trying her best to process the events that occurred. What a nightmare she'll always remember.

"What's that in the distance?" Billy asked.

Annie turns to look at what's caught Billy's attention. A thick black column of smoke emerges from the buildings covering parts of the gorgeous pink sunset, an orange blaze follows underneath. They can feel heat burn in the atmosphere, any closer they would be sweating. Within seconds the screaming of the townsfolk erupts.

"We've got to get there now!" Annie screeches.

Billy runs alongside Annie without hesitation. The nearer they ran to the village the less they could see. The smoke has blacked out the streets. People scream bumping into each other.

"What happened?" Billy asks a nearby stranger.

"At first, a fire broke out at the church, and then one broke out at the stables it's a nightmare!"

"The stables? The horses!" Annie dashes to the outside of town to the stables. The fire burns through the wood; the barn is not going to last much longer. The horse's shriek in utter panic, they are trapped.

"Billy! Help me with this!"

The pair sprint to the double doors of the barn, but it's locked.

"Who has the keys?" Billy asks.

The sweat pours down their faces as they race against time. A pitchfork leans on the hay bale. Jackson must have just left it there instead of putting it back to where it's supposed to be, but for this one occasion, they are glad he didn't. Billy uses the pitchfork to smash the lock on the doors. The smoke and blaze knock the pair back, it'll be dangerous, but they're not leaving until every horse is freed. The horses continue to shriek and jump but hopefully its comfort that they know their riders are here to save them. Lifting the hooks on every stable door the gates fling open and the horses charge to freedom.

"Everyone's out, let's go!"

As Annie makes a dash for it, debris falls from the roof and lands near Annie, knocking her sideways. She falls and hits her head on stable door, knocking herself out.

The authorities do their utmost to escort everyone from the villages to safer grounds; they spread across the outskirts of the town as the fire shows no mercy.

The sky is no longer pink; it's pure black.

"She'll be okay; she just needs to rest. She's lucky you were there to help her out to safety."

Annie slowly opens her eyes; she's away from it all.

"Thank god you're okay," Billy puts his arm around her.

Annie reaches to touch her head but ouch!

"Yeah, you might have a nasty bump."

Annie looks to the hills where a tall dark figure stands watching over at the total devastation. He's too far away for her to identify who it is. He turns in the other direction and soon disappears into the forests.

KATHY'S

Settling down with a glass of Pinot Grigio beside her Annie switched on the radio. Unusually for a Friday night, the town centre was quiet and empty. Living in the middle of town could be an advantage, but sometimes it had its downside. Not tonight, however, thought Annie. I will be able to listen to the radio in peace.

As the soothing strains of Mozart echoed in the silent room, Annie took a sip of wine and settled into her favourite armchair.

Without warning a brilliant light suddenly lit up the night sky invading the room. As Annie looked out of the window, she gasped at what she saw. Rubbing her eyes in disbelief, she looked again, but no, there it was a huge, a spherical object floating in the sky. She watched fascinated as it drifted silently down, landing in her back garden.

Almost against her will, Annie found herself walking into the garden, moving towards the saucer-shaped object and the open door.

As she entered the door, two androgynous creatures drew her close. Annie had never seen anything like them. Green amorphous shapes with huge protruding eyes and antenna where ears should have been.

Instead of feeling frightened, Annie felt strangely safe as they protectively walked her towards a third creature who sat on a throne. The two beings bowed and moved back as the creature spoke in a high-pitched voice.

"Don't be frightened Annie, we mean you no harm we would just like to ask you a few questions. Go with the others who will take care of you.".

Annie woke suddenly to the voice of the BBC Announcer, "We hope you've enjoyed your evening of Mozart. Tune in next week when we will be featuring the works of Johann Sebastian Bach."

Annie rubbed her eyes and stared at the clock. 9.30 pm. Where had the last three hours gone? Her glass of wine lay virtually untouched. I've had a weird dream she thought I must have fallen asleep straight away, "Never had a dream quite like that! I must have been tired, and now I've missed the whole concert."

As she drew the curtains, Annie's eyes were drawn towards the garden. All was silent, but there was no doubting the brown saucer shape mark scorched into the otherwise green lawn.

She reared back in horror and moved quickly onto the chair. It must have been a dream; these things don't happen in real life; there are no such things as aliens. She racked her brains, trying to remember, but all she could recall of her dream was the creatures.

As Annie tried to convince herself that nothing odd had occurred, she knew that whatever had transpired that evening, it had been a night to remember.

BAILEY'S

"What a night to remember," sighed Annie as she began to recall her eventful evening.

Annie and her boyfriend Liam were out in the town centre that was alive with noise. There was excitement in the air as this was their first date night in a few months as they both have extremely inflexible working hours. They made their way to their favourite club where they planned to dance and drink all night long as that's their favourite way to let their hair down.

Relaxing and dancing together made them fall for each other all over again. Annie felt the butterflies in her stomach again like it was the first time they met. She hadn't felt that happy in a while. They started to leave to spend the rest of the night cuddled up on the sofa, and as Annie came out of the bathroom to where Liam was waiting to go, she saw him in a heated argument with a woman she hadn't seen before. All Annie heard before being spotted was, "I've told you to stay away from her, Harley. I don't want you being friends with her."

They went home, Annie feeling unsettled by the exchange she witnessed and began to watch a movie with the noisy background sounds of the town centre outside. Only moments had past when Annie couldn't help but ask, "Who is Harley?" as she had a bad gut feeling of her boyfriend not being faithful.

Liam explained that she was nothing but a co-worker who keeps asking to meet Annie, but Liam doesn't trust her intentions.

An hour later there was a knock at the door but when Annie opened it there was no one there. An envelope and a single red rose laid on the doorstep, so she slowly picked it up. Her eyes scanned the note that read, "Hi Annie, you looked good tonight. Would you mind giving me a call? My number is below. I'm sure I can make you happier than that lazy man you currently have. Love, H"

"What a night to remember," Annie thought again as she sent a text to the number while her unknowing boyfriend slept beside her.

VICKI'S

Annie sat watching TV; it was Friday night, and her favourite show was just about to start. She had looked forward to seeing it all week; it's about how a vampire was trying to live life as a 'normal' person. She watched every show that she could about vampire's- she loved them, they intrigued her.

Loud noises outside on the street started to make her angry; it was disturbing her enjoyment! She liked living right in the town centre: except on Friday and Saturday nights when all the town idiots congregated at the 'in' place to be, which just happened to be just down the road from her flat.

Suddenly a loud piercing scream filled the air. It sounded so full of pain that it unsettled Annie enough that she got up to check out of the window. She realised that it hadn't come from the front of her flat as usual, as that window overlooking the main road. No, the scream had come from the back, which overlooked the service area for the shops located under her flat.

As she pulled back the curtain, there was another toe-curling scream, and that's when she spotted them, a couple standing against a wall canoodling. Except that wasn't what was happening, the man was, in fact, biting the side of the lady's neck. Blood was coming out of the bite marks, and as he let go of the lady, she slumped to the floor and Annie couldn't help but let out a loud gasp.

The man looked up at her window and Annie took in the blood around his mouth was also covering his sharp teeth. Their eyes met and held. Annie didn't look away; she held his gaze as a smile formed on her lips.

'This is not a usual reaction,' David thought, as the lady at the window just continued to stare. His feasting already forgotten, David whisked himself to the front door of the intriguing lady and knocked.

Within seconds she had opened the door and held it open, inviting him in.

"Are you sure?" he asked, giving her the chance to refuse him. Vampires have to be invited in after all.

"Absolutely," she replied, surprisingly with excitement, rather than fear.

David stepped into her flat and allowed her to lead the way to her front room, where she indicated for him to sit.

"I'm Annie," she said.

"I'm David."

"I'm so pleased to meet you. I always knew Vampires were real; I just knew it!"

David didn't know quite what to say. He had never been in this position before. Not only did she intrigue him, but he had never been drawn or attracted to a human woman before. So, he did something that he had never done before; he sat and spent time just chatting. They talked for hours, neither realising the passage of time. They agreed on some topics and argued on others.

The night gave way to day and the day turned into evening. They only stopped talking to eat and drink. Then as night again came, David took Annie's hand and led her to her bed. He was so surprised at himself; was it possible to fall in love so quickly and so deeply?

They made love wildly and passionately until they were both exhausted and fell asleep, entwined around each other.

Several hours later, David left the flat conflicted and full of regret. Up in her flat, Annie lay on her bed, lifeless. It appears that a vampire's urge for blood is stronger than the stirrings of a new love.

KEV'S

Annie was unsettled; she couldn't stop fidgeting and just relax. There seems to be an abundance of traffic and noise outside her small one-bedroom house today. She was too hungover to rise and see what's happening; her eyes tired and heavy sent her back to sleep.

Annie awoke roughly an hour later, and the noise was not getting any quieter.

"What the hell is happening out there?" she muttered to herself. Unsteady on her legs, she slowly went to her kitchen and started to make a cup of tea.

On the way back to her Saint Anne comfy chair, she decided to go to the window and see what the palaver was all about. There were several Police vans and two ambulances in the street, and a yellow taped cordon was around her friend Leigh's house.

"Oh shit, I hope Leigh is okay," she says aloud to nobody in particular.

On opening the door, she saw a young female cop, who was about to knock.

"Can I help you, dear?" she inquired.

"I hope so," the female replied.

"There has been a nasty incident next door, did you happen to hear anything last night?"

"I was in with Leigh drinking until about one," Annie said.

The female cop asked if it was okay to send in a detective to talk to her and Annie agreed.

Detective Arthur Clew showed Annie his warrant card and entered the house, and Annie told him to sit and asked if he would like a cup of tea, which he declined.

"Can you tell me everything you remember about last night, please?" he asked. She told him what she could bring to mind from last night and then sat there looking blank.

Her eyes started to water as she began remembering more now; she coughed, and tears flowed in streams now.

"It was just after midnight; we were very drunk. Leigh and her friend Steve decided to take the piss out of me, and I got furious. I picked up the nearest bottle and struck Steve on the head. He went down on the floor and then with the shattered glass I stabbed him in the neck, Leigh screamed a silent scream, so I hit her hard with my fist. In the corner of the room was a heavy brass ornament, I picked it up and hit Leigh's head several times. She lay there not moving, and I had a cigarette and another drink. Then I swore I heard Leigh call me a stupid cow, so I walked over to her and jumped up and pogo'ed on her head roughly ten times. It was when I felt moistness seeping into my shoe, that I stopped. Steve, at this time, was still gurgling, the noise began to become annoying, so I kicked his head quite a few times until he completely stopped moving. I then needed to clean up, so I had a shower in Leigh's, then came home and fell asleep. I blacked it all out until now, and I am so sorry".

When Annie had finished her story, there were three more police officers in the room listening. She just looked at the floor crying even harder now. Detective Arthur Clew put handcuffs on her and then covered them with a coat as he walked her to the car.

JONATHAN'S

I desperately wanted to get away from being 'Little Orphan Annie.' I was tired of people feeling sorry for me and excluding me from their plans. I suppose I was a wet rag. I could put the mockers on the most glorious events if I were allowed to. How could I break out of my shell and be the real me?

My therapist said I would feel better if I changed the way I looked. I was so used to having the same hairstyle, and I didn't want to pay for ripped jeans. Why would anyone? I wasn't wasteful, but I disposed of any torn clothes I couldn't repair. I suppose that was part of my problem. I wanted to live in the past. "If it's not broke, why fix it?" seemed to be my mantra. That was probably why many of my colleagues lost interest in me. Not only was I boring, but I was also unwilling to try anything new. I didn't like modern life. I preferred watching old films from my childhood – no explicit sex and bad language. I had an imagination and could also assess what people would say and do, rather than being told.

I decided that I shall change my appearance tomorrow. I booked appointments at "Hair low, Dolly" and my local John Lewis store, where a stylist will determine which clothes would be most appropriate based on my height, age, complexion and the like. I had read that most people are unaware of what they really look like. I also intended to visit the make-up counter to determine how to make myself look more attractive. It all seemed so false, but I had to make a new start in life in order to free myself from my current restraints. I had enough money to fulfil my dreams, and if I didn't use it to make myself feel better, what was the point of having it?

It's very noisy out there. It's just as well that I'm all alone in my flat. I can hear the alarm at the local supermarket and the siren of emergency vehicles. I'm glad I'm such a boring person. Nobody will link me to the incident, even if they bang on the door.

"Can I help you?"

"Sorry ma'am, we were looking for a dangerous criminal."

All I need to do is to last out the night. Tomorrow, I'll be a new person.

No longer 'Little Orphan Annie'. Now 'Annie, get your gun'.

MARK'S

In a noisy town, on a quiet night, Annie was unsettled as always. Why was it so quiet?

But it wasn't quiet for long as there was a loud booming knock at her door. She opens it ready to tell the idiot from across the hall, or her loser boyfriend, that she hasn't been stealing her milk, but it wasn't her at the door, it was a big man in a beard.

He forces his way in and says that he's a prison escapee and he wants to stay the night to hide out. Annie is now in full unsettled mode and potters about all over her front room. "Want some tea?" she asks.

"Coffee," the man replied. So, she made him a coffee, and he told her all about how he didn't kill that man and that it was all an accident. Annie was scared, yeah, but most people don't want to chat to her long as she is so unsettled all the time. It was then that Annie knew that he couldn't leave, so while he was going to the toilet, she called the police. Unsettled Annie had company; at last, she was so happy.

A few hours later and they had had a lovely evening and a really good chat, even a laugh. Annie is finally feeling settled; it's a good feeling for her.

Then she says, "I want you to escape."

The crook replies, "I have no chance."

Then Annie comes up with a plan; she exits her flat and makes her way to the flat across the hall. She knocks out the women who lives there and hides the crook there. The police burst in a few hours later and knocked at the house that the crook was now in. He was wearing the lady's clothes, and he had shaved. They showed them around and said that the women were her sister and after the police had gone Annie and the crook parted ways.

From that day on, Annie was a confident lady, and she moved to a lovely new house in a quiet town and got an excellent job. The crook, well, he was caught a few days later, but for Annie, it wasn't about whether he got away. The lady next door never accused her of stealing her milk again; in fact, she apologised to her for it. Annie had a good life all because of that night that she will never forget. The night a crook, whose name she never got, come to stay, who she helped escape and she finally got revenge on that horrible women across the hall.　　She eventually becomes just Annie.

SKY'S PROMPT

SHE PULLED THE DAGGER FROM HER BACK AND LAUGHED, "YOU FORGOT SOMETHING."

ABOUT SKY

Hey there! My name is Sky Kelly. I started writing four years ago since attending my Creative Writing group. I prefer to play sports than watching it. I enjoy all music. I love writing rhyming poetry and short stories. I'd love to write comedy one day, but as we all know, humour is subjective. I like to read graphic novels, mystery, comedy and crime novels.

SKY'S

She pulled the dagger
straight from her back,
but the blood wasn't red
it was an eerie black.

It wasn't her blood
the poison rests on the knife,
sliding down the edge
trying to take her life.

Looking at the blade
she sees her reflection,
and then the face
that offered false protection.

Clutching the weapon
adding it to the collection,
a valuable lesson
she learned deception.

Revenge leaves her seething
slithers in her veins,
dealing with this problem
it's all that remains.

Sharpening the knife
she plans her attack,
karma is a bitch
when you stab me in the back.

She utters the words
'your time will come',
and when it does
you'll be left so numb.

The tears that fall
murder flares in her eyes,
there's no going back
as he's in for a surprise.

He left her behind
so she'd take the fall,
crashing to the ground
standing over her so tall.

"It's nothing personal,"
as he grabs the money,
"it's just business
see you soon, honey."

This was his fault
the robbery went wrong,
but she knows now
he strung her along.

He reveals the dagger
and black liquid drips,
her life now hangs
right at his fingertips.

The poison burns
piercing her back,
she screams in distress
from the awful flashback.

She finds him hiding
cowering in the hut,
closing the curtains
with the doors locked shut.

Throwing the Molotov
the cabin ignites,
the blazing orange
illumines the night.

He makes a run for it
he knows she's here,
with the thick smoke on his side
he's certain he'll disappear.

Releasing the arrow
it strikes his leg,
screaming to the ground
now to watch him beg.

Completely at her mercy
he can no longer run,
the blood pours on the snow
what has he done?

Emerging from the smoke
a smile on her face,
it was easier than she thought
not putting up a chase.

Revealing the dagger
karmas come back around,
piercing his heart
crows flee from the sound.

Life leaves his body
he takes his last breath,
looking to the sky
as he welcomes death.

She falls back in the snow
breathing a sigh of relief,
she can now move on
from all this hurt and grief.

KATHY'S

The poster was freshly pasted on the theatre wall, 'Coming soon The Great Suprendo - magic and Illusions to thrill and amaze you. Tickets £13.50 Seniors and students £10.00.'

Katie had always loved magic and was excited when she saw the poster on her way home from college. She would ask Rick if he wanted to go with her. Maybe Mum would stand her the tenner. After all, she didn't get out much and had done so well in her last exams.

The Great Suprendo had not been having a great time of it lately. Things had been difficult with him and Sophie, and he could not imagine how they would cope with what she had done. As far as he was concerned, the marriage was over. His love for her had turned to near hatred. The big problem was that she was not only his wife she was also his assistant. The show must go on, but he was struggling to smile on stage with the bitterness inside him.

Paul Matthews, another magician on the circuit, had died recently and Jenny his partner was eager to join him. Paul's act had not been dissimilar to his, and it would be easy to show her his own tricks. But Sophie was not having any of it. Unless he paid her off to the tune of £100,000, she was going nowhere.

There was no way he could afford that kind of money, and she knew it, and even if he could there was no way she was blackmailing him into a split. It was as he was throwing the knife at Sophie on the Wednesday Matinee that the idea came to him. Why he had not thought of it before he didn't know, it would be so easy to substitute the dummy knife, Sophie would never believe he could be that wicked.

Saturday night and the theatre was packed. Tension built up in the theatre as the finale approached and The Great Soprando donned the blindfold. Katie sat enthralled as the knife flew through the air towards his assistant. A loud gasp erupted from the audience as the scantily clad assistant slumped to the floor. The whole of the theatre fell silent as the curtain came down.

Behind the scenes, The Great Soprando rushed towards his wife. As he reached the body, Sophie turned and pulled the dagger from her back and whispered: "You forgot something. I told you that you talk in your sleep, but you never believed me." He slumped to the floor as her laugh echoed throughout the theatre.

"How was your evening, mum?" asked Katie.
"Well, it was certainly different," she replied.

BAILEY'S

"You forgot something," Amanda Clark said as a twisted smile played upon her lips," what would you do without me?"

A deep laugh echoed into the house as Amanda's husband, Harry, came back to take the dagger out of her hand where it seemed not to belong. The dagger is a 'just in case' tool; he's never had to use it. Harry swooped down and gave her a kiss to show his gratitude.

Harry had never met a woman like Amanda. She's a perfect picture: slim body, curves in all the right places, silky long blonde hair. She looks as though she's strutted straight out of a magazine. As he left the house, he felt grateful to have found a woman so unbelievably perfect for him that she even understood his need to steal under the blanket of darkness that night brings.

As the front door softly shut, Amanda sighed then headed straight to her walk-in wardrobe and discarded herself from her baby pink pyjamas and matching slippers into something more appropriate for work. Tonight, party wear is needed but nothing that stands out as she mustn't be remembered. She slipped into a black skin-tight jumpsuit that showed just enough cleavage to ensure things go her way. She delicately tied her into a bun, she hated how long it was, but Harry liked it, and finally, she put on her favourite black boots as who would wear heels? They make too much noise. Ready, she left the house via the backdoor in case of any prying neighbours were around. She headed towards her assignment location, her local night club.

Amanda sat on the leather barstool, Whiskey Sour in her hand as she spotted him amongst the sweaty bodies on the dance floor. Flicking through her phone, she double-checked the photo she was sent just in case she was wrong. She wasn't. It was him. Smoothly she made her way through the crowd with her deep blue eyes locked onto him. They danced, and she whispered sweet lies until she knew the time was right. He agreed to go into the alley - they always agree.

He was drunk, and she was sober. Her hand found and then unbuckled his belt. He smiled. Before he knew it, she had the belt tight in her grips, and it was wrapped professionally around his neck. When the body finally stopped fighting back and wriggling around, Amanda carefully laid it on the damp floor. With a now gloved hand, she pushed his hair off of his forehead and made him look comfortable. That's when she leant forward, lips close to his ear, and whispered, "Number 65".

Gracefully she joined the party for another few hours as leaving straight away would be suspicious, but she left with enough time to be home for Harry's arrival.

Dressed back in her fluffy pink pyjamas, Amanda waited for her unknowing husband to return from his night of childish mischief.

The next morning Amanda woke up to the smell of her favourite coffee and a kiss on her cheek from the love of her life. Beside her, her phone lit up. It read, "New assignment: Harry Clark, £1,000". A taste of blood filled her mouth as she got up to give her handsome husband one last kiss.

VICKI'S

Ruby looked down from her penthouse over the people and properties that she owned. Nearly the whole neighbourhood belonged to her now and the parts that didn't, well, she would see to it that soon she would.

She brushed her long black hair up into a ponytail to get it out of her way as she sat at her desk to read her mail that had been delivered a short while ago.

Most people would find her office oppressive, but she didn't. Everything was either jet black or blood red, the same as her clothing. She didn't own any clothes that weren't black or red. With her black hair, it made her look pale and lifeless; even her eyes were very dark. She often heard people talk about her behind her back, remarking how her eyes were dead and soulless, just like her. She didn't care. She didn't need people to like her, only to obey her.

Ruby opened up her first letter. It was from the manager of one of the apartment blocks that she owned. Apparently, the place was in such disrepair that the mould on the walls was causing the elderly and the young to become ill. He was begging her for some money to make some repairs. Ruby tore the letter up. The mould didn't affect her, so it was of no consequence.

The next letter was from the manager of a parade of shops that she owned. Ruby had bought five shops a few months ago: a café, sweetshop, convenience store, dry cleaners and a fish 'n' chip shop. The manager she had hired was meant to run all five without bothering her, so she didn't bother reading the whole boring thing, she just skim read…. low wages…. quick turnover…. poor working conditions. Again, as it didn't affect her, the letter went straight into the bin.

Bored of reading all of the begging letters Ruby decided to head out. She called her driver and told him to be outside pronto; she wasn't to be kept waiting. Ruby left the building, and as she opened the car door, she saw movement out of the corner of her eye. A lady was running straight towards her shouting 'This is for my dad', and the next thing she knew, she had a dagger sticking out of her back.

She pulled the dagger out from her back and laughed, "You forgot something." She said as she handed it back to the lady. Ruby grabbed the lady by her front and pulled her close so that she could look into her eyes. Their eyes locked and the lady couldn't look away, she tried, but her head just didn't respond to her anymore. Deep in Ruby's eyes, the lady saw what she truly was, and she started to scream a terrifying scream. In her eye, she saw Hell.

Ruby pushed the lady to the floor and walked back to her car and, as she got in, she looked back and winked.

The lady was now one of a few who could see Ruby in her true form; the spell disguising her was broken. She soon became known as 'The Mad Lady' as she roamed the streets daily warning everyone that the devil lived amongst them in the form of a woman who felt no pain and just laughed when she got stabbed in the back and did nothing in return except wink.

KEV'S

We used to be very close; as close as twins. She shared my clothes and makeup, and I used hers. Our birthdays are in the same month, so when growing up we made sure we had one big party. Both our hairstyles were the same, and we wore very similar clothes. When T.J, Chaz, Seb and Lee chucked her; I was the shoulder for her to cry on. I was slightly bigger than Kayleigh, and more of a scrapper. In secondary school, when she was being bullied, I stuck up for her and got suspended for attacking the bullies.

People had always had to invite Kayleigh and Sharona together for social events. We were known as the Dagenham Duo. Then that fateful night out changed everything. A night that started out as one of the best of our young lives- and ended up as a complete nightmare.

We were at the Trampoline Arena; there was seven of us having fun before Kayleigh's wedding to Ashley. I accidentally jumped onto Kayleigh's back while she was jumping, and I heard her neck crack; she collapsed straight away, screaming out in agony. She had broken her neck and ended up in a wheelchair. The weeks after were the worst; tears from both of us and lots of frustration from her.

The wedding was called off, and Ashley left her. Her friends slowly disappeared, and I moved further and further away from her.

One day six years later, I was walking along Valence Avenue and bumped into Kayleigh being pushed by a very handsome man. They stopped, and she introduced

Simon as her husband. We made small talk, she asked how I was keeping, and I explained that I was single, jobless and living in a local bedsit.

Simon and Kayleigh now live in Gidea Park, in a four bedroomed house. A Mercedes in the drive and they got married in St Lucia.

She said she didn't blame me for her injury; it was a pure accident. But was more upset that everybody left her, and worse was the fact her friend, who was like a sister; me had drifted away.

She reminisced about the old days, and we laughed, then she mentioned ex-boyfriends. I gulped at the thought of them.

"I know you slept with all my ex-boyfriends. You could never pull you own one."

"I am so so sorry, Kay; it just happened, if I could turn back time I would."

"Just save your breath, Sharona," she snapped, "you knew what you were doing, and enjoyed it."

She rose out of the chair; I stood gob smacked, as she reached behind her and said, "This dagger you put in my back, you can have it back now."

They both laughed as they walked off, leaving me in tears.

JONATHAN'S

Sandra used to enjoy working at the circus, apart from the clowns. They weren't funny at all. They were a bit creepy, and she didn't know why people laughed if one of them had a custard pie thrown in his face or the doors fell off his car. Sandra couldn't afford a decent car and would have preferred the circus to buy her a new car, rather than keep paying for cars that fell apart.

Sandra used to like working with the big cats, but even that had begun to pall. She realised that the lions and tigers didn't have enough space to move about within their cages. Their only exercise was within the circus ring, and then they were expected to jump through hoops, sometimes singeing their fur on the flames. It seemed cruel, and Sandra was glad that the circus would soon be prevented from exploiting wild animals and she would no longer see a chained elephant outside the circus tent.

Sandra entered the manager's office.

"We are concerned about your lack of enthusiasm at the circus. Some of the customers have complained about your surly attitude and your negative comments about your work. While you are here, you represent the circus company that pays your wages. The customers want to enjoy themselves and don't want to be distracted by a grumpy employee. Some customers have told me that you have complained about the treatment of the animals and about how we force dolls' clothes on the monkeys. What you think about that is up to you, but you are being disloyal when you complain to the customers who pay towards your wages. The less money we get, the less there will be for the staff. If the circus closes down, you will be out of a job and don't expect me to give you a decent reference. As far as I'm concerned, you are one of the reasons why attendance figures are down. I don't know how many people you've complained to, but if each one tells someone else; things will get worse for us. I can't prove it was you, but the article in yesterday's 'Daily Informer' was based on inside information and couldn't have been guessed by the journalist. I could sack you here and now, but I can't trust you, and I suspect that if you blabber to the press, that could be the end of my career. I'm going to give you one last chance. Samaldi, the magician, needs a new assistant."

Sandra quite liked Samaldi. Despite his false moustache, he was more genuine than most of the others. He was one of the old-fashioned magicians. There was no point in doing card tricks in the big tent. Nobody could see them and was it really worth it to buy big screens to show that a stooge had chosen the Ace of Diamonds or whatever?

Samaldi was involved in a show-stopper routine. Sandra looked glamorous for a change as she was attached to a large spinning wheel and Samaldi threw daggers at her. She was more bothered about a dagger cutting through a strap on her gown, rather than entering her heart. It was unlikely that Samaldi would be that accurate even if he hadn't been wearing a blindfold. Samaldi threw daggers at various angles, including backwards, and used techniques that would have made a bowler wince. How could he do this if he couldn't see the target?

Eventually, all the daggers had been cast, and Samaldi bowed to the ecstatic audience. Sandra was still attached to the wheel. Why hadn't she joined him on the podium? He looked at her. Her arm reached out, and she pulled the dagger from her back and laughed.

"You forgot something."

MARK'S

The queen who couldn't die
but that didn't stop me try.
From seven stories she did fly,
When she shrugged it off, I wanted to cry.
I even poisoned a sweet apple pie,
And still, the queen wouldn't die.
I went for it one day with a knife I couldn't do anything
She pulled the knife from her back and said you forgot something,
And she threw it my way like an arrow; it sped,
If I could have moved, I would have fled,
But now unlike the queen, I am dead.
For years and years, she reined,
The resources of the land were drained,
Her head collection never lost; only gained.
Then one day a young boy,
Found a new toy,
And screamed with joy,
For he was the first in the village to speak,
Late one night into her chamber he did sneak,
And bellowed out 'Queen I want you to die.'
He no longer had to try,
She went slowly with a tear in her eye,
Now the boy who could speak taught it to the land,
When they learned, they found him quite bland.
So, his head in the room they added,
And the king and queen one by one got beheaded,
For a land who couldn't kill a horrible leader,
Now are all that much meaner.
The need to decide quick,
Or they will get a massive kick,
From a country who wants to take them over,

Then one day a girl found a clover,
And wished for it she had to try,
A return of the Queen who couldn't die.
With a flash and a bang, she appeared,
And the threat of war disappeared,
And so, the cycle goes on.
Maybe one day,
They can do it alone, come what may,
I think it will be a Tuesday.

EMILY'S

Marly spent a year of her life while working as a photographic apprentice with a young man named Adam. They met up frequently, and she was in love for the first time aged twenty- three. Due to his erratic behaviour of late, she was unsure of their future together. Sometimes he wouldn't show up at planned dates. Optimistic overall, she accepted his apologies. 'One last chance I will allow him,' she thought on their next meeting.

Adam appeared different not only in his outfit but also his mood. He was sarcastic and openly unpleasant.

'Enough is enough,' she thought and said," Adam, sorry to say this, but I want to call a halt to our relationship." An argument followed with him shouting abuse. Then he left slamming the front door.

That night Marly had a nightmare, waking up sweating, shaking, sobbing remembering a knife being plunged in her back by Adam. Realising she needed to talk to someone, she rang her friend Susie, a detective.

"You may think I am losing my marbles, but this dream has unnerved me!"

"Let's chat more Marly, call a cab and come over to me."

Within the hour, the dream, plus Adam's erratic behaviour was relayed.

"I have a plan for tomorrow, Marly. Call and arrange to meet Adam at your home. In the meantime, I will have a police officer check on him."

Adam agreed and arrived forty- five minutes late, no apology. He was aggressive in manner, and Marly was inwardly shaking. As she stood at the kitchen sink, he came up behind her saying, "No one leaves me you bitch, who do you think you are, Lady Muck take that."

Marly felt something pushing through her back and screamed: "Help!" Whereupon the front door was smashed in revealing three police officers, who grabbed Adam and forced him to the ground, handcuffing him.

As Adam got up, Marly pulled the dagger from her back and laughed saying, " You forgot something, you idiot," as she handed it to Susie, who came from the room next door, bagging it.

"I followed my omen, and we were ready for you. I knew the creepy stunt you planned. Little did you know I would have on padded protection. I screamed for back up, not out of pain."

It transpired after the investigation that Adam's change in personality was due to him being a drug-dealing gangster and heroin addict. All that in the space of a few months. Sad but true.

NATALIE'S PROMPT

YOU ARE WALKING HOME FROM A HEAVY NIGHT ON THE TOWN WITH FRIENDS. IT IS AROUND 4 AM. YOU ARE ALONE WITH BOTH A FUZZY HEAD AND LACK OF MEMORY ABOUT WHAT HAS HAPPENED TOWARDS THE END OF THE NIGHT. YOU REALISE AFTER A WHILE THAT YOUR CLOTHES ARE RIPPED AND THERE IS A LARGE CUT ON YOUR KNEE. EVENTUALLY, YOU MAKE IT HOME TO SEE THAT YOUR FRONT DOOR HAS BEEN KICKED IN. WHAT HAPPENS NEXT?

ABOUT NATALIE

Natalie was our facilitator when we were run by Green Shoes Arts. It was a significant loss to our group when she left as she was more than a teacher but a friend too. It was Natalie who inspired us with confidence and made us the group that we are today. We miss her!

KATHY'S

January 1st, 1998

All was dark in the road as Sophie approached her house. Quite how she had got there, she didn't know. The fuzziness in her head was making her feel sick and totally disorientated.

She looked at her watch; 4.30 am? How did her dress get ripped, how did she get the large cut on her knee? She was so frightened- she couldn't remember anything after that last gin. She knew she must get inside her house, try to recall her movements in the Club.

Scrabbling around in her bag she found her keys, but a jolt of fear ran through her, the door had been kicked in. Her last recollection was of the hand clasped over her mouth and the sickly smell.

As she awoke in the cold dark cellar despair enveloped her. Tears running down her cheeks, she banged and shouted out, but all she could hear was her voice echoing in the stillness.

When he opened the cellar door, he was smiling. "I've brought you some food." Staring into the deep brown eyes, she remembered.

"You're the man who bought me that last drink at the Club. Who are you? What do you want? Please let me go."

"I'm sorry I can't do that, but you're safe with me. I won't harm you; I just want to look after you."

The 6 o'clock news announcement was terse. Fears are growing over the disappearance of Sophie Rawlings last seen leaving Pulse Nightclub on Saturday evening at 3.30 am. When she disappeared, blonde, blue-eyed Sophie was wearing a black dress and matching the black jacket with rose motif. She has a small butterfly tattoo on her right wrist.

Enquiries at her house revealed it to be empty, the last sighting of her by a neighbour was 7.15 pm on Saturday evening. The police were alerted by work colleagues when she did not turn up on Monday.

"Sophie is very reliable," said her boss. "She would never not turn up without ringing in. We are very concerned."

Friends and family are devastated by her disappearance, which is totally out of character. Anyone who has any information, please call the Police number on the screen in strictest confidence.

February 2nd, 2008

BBC Breaking news. "At 8.30am this morning a woman walked into Weston Police Station purporting to be Sophie Rawlings, the 22-year-old who went missing on 1st January 1988 after visiting a Nightclub with friends. Despite a nationwide appeal at the time and thousands of police hours spent searching, nothing has been heard of Sophie since that date.

The distraught woman claims she was captured by a man who drugged her in the Nightclub and has forcibly held her in his cellar since then. Sophie is currently being interviewed at Weston Police station, and her family have been informed. Officers are interviewing a man at an address in the village of Comber. We will bring you news of this incredible story as it unfolds.

Jonathon Briggs, BBC News."

KEV'S

"What a night!" I thought to myself — a jigsaw puzzle of what has happened flitters through my mind.

It's now 4 am, and all my friends have disappeared to their homes, I'm glad Tommy enjoyed his stag night.

As I approach my house I look down and see a rip in my jeans and my knee has a cut, blood is oozing down my leg. I realised I am limping. I look up and see my front door has been kicked in. I grab a milk bottle from the doorstep and creep into my hallway. Standing still I listen out for any noise; all I hear is my own rapid heartbeat.

The front room is empty, but there is furniture overturned and smashed bottles on the floor. I move on to my bedroom and open the door as slow and as quietly as I can. My bed is a mess, which is natural, but the room is okay. My kitchen, however, is a different matter, glasses everywhere, cupboards all ajar, food spilt everywhere and blood on the floor.

After my call to the police, I sat down on my doorstep with my mind in turmoil. Not being able to focus on what occurred was annoying me. A police car pulls up about fifteen minutes later, and I explain that I think I've been burgled and I'm still fuzzy with my memory after a bender.

They took their time going through my house, and while they were doing the search, I started to remember.

Cliff and Richard came over early, and we got into the drink right away, we downed a bottle of vodka and whisky between us. Rich was being boisterous and seemed to be on something. In the kitchen Rich became aggressive, and he started to wreck my kitchen. Cliff and I tried to stop him, and at one point, he pushed me onto the floor, and that's when I cut my knee.

Rich left abruptly, and I was so pissed and angry that I wrecked my own front room. I told Cliff we should still go and enjoy the stag night. We left my house, and I realised I had left my keys indoors, so I kicked in the door and collected them, then we set off for a night of drink and fun.

With my tail between my legs, I had to go and tell the police, I'm sorry, but their time was wasted and that it was a night of fun that turned out wrong.

JONATHAN'S

"Where am I?" That's a cliché, but it's how I feel as I wake up. I had dreamt of lying beneath my duvet, but I realise I am lying on a pavement. I feel cold and lonely. The full moon looks down at me. Is it being condescending, or does it pity me? It is 4.32, obviously a.m. At least I retain some sense of logic. I must have got here somehow. I struggle to my feet and brush myself down. Wait a minute. My clothes are ripped and not in the most discrete place...

It seems that a sledgehammer is beating on my brain. My right knee has a large scab, probably covering a deep cut. What has happened to me? I open a pocket and extract some cards. At least I know where I live and know how to get there. I just can't recollect the last few hours. I walk down my road and see that my front door has been kicked in. If I were more awake, I'd have a panic attack, but it seems that this is just another case of something going wrong in my life, but why me?

Should I enter my house or call 999? Which is more important – the police or ambulance? I don't know if the cut is infected or what caused it. I decide to go in, get changed and have a hot drink to clear my head. Everywhere I go, I feel I'm being watched. Perhaps I'm paranoid, but wouldn't you be? Why did people pick on me, rip my clothes, cut my knee and kick in my front door? Are the incidents related? I know someone who blames herself for the bad things that happen in her life, even though that isn't logical. I've been doing that for years; it's almost as if I'm my worst enemy. As I look around, I hear my washing machine. Somebody must have removed my clothes from the floor. The cut on my right knee has healed. Surely it couldn't do that in two hours.

I wake up as the washing machine stops and the door opens. My clothes emerge and walk down the corridor. I follow. I suppose that if someone wanted to rob my house, they would have done so by now, not that there was much worth stealing. The clothes lead me back to the pavement where I had been left. The area is cordoned off, and a chalk outline showed where I had rested. My clothes nod reverently at the figure and return to face me. I am overcome by the life I have lost and can never recover. I return home, and there is a new door and a notice. "Trespassers will be prosecuted." Could I a trespasser in my own home? I cuddle my clothes. They are my only friends.

MARK'S

What has happened? I'm standing at my front door; my clothes are ripped, and my knee is cut. What happened to me? To make a bad night worse; the front door has been kicked in, and it's a mess in there.

I enter to see what's missing; the living room first. There is blood everywhere, and my mum and dad are lying on the sofa, eyes open, dead! I close their eyes. I'm a mess; what happened here?

I have to go and look further. Each room I go into has a different family member in there, and they are all dead. There is a note on the wall in blood, 'You think you can mess with us.' What was going on here?

I hear a noise behind me, and a fight breaks out between a man and me. He is saying sorry as I kick him in his joy department. I quickly get a chair, and some duct tape and I tie him up; I will have answers.

I get some of dad's tools and drag the guy to Julie's room; it's the only one that's available. After a few hours, the guy had spilt his guts about how on my night out they thought I was some Russian spy. They stole my driving licence and decided to wipe out my family and have the 'chair man' here to get me upon my return. They even spiked my drink so I wouldn't be on my game when I arrive. Funny what seeing everyone you love dead can do! I get his phone and on it is a list of names; the ones who made this mistake; the ones who needed to pay for this, starting with this guy here. But what to use? I search around the house looking for something to use; this guy had to suffer.

Then out the corner of my eye, in the corner, a pogo stick. I whack the guy over the head, knocking him out cold, and I lay him down on his back. I get on the pogo stick and begin to bounce; I jump really high and eventually plunge it deep into this guy's chest, killing him instantly.

Now I need a new identity; a new life; I have a purpose; to find the people on my list. My family is dead, but I'm not. All I need is a few kills, and I'm done, then I can get on with my life. It was on this day, after a few drinks with friends and a case of mistaken identity, that the pogo killer was created, and this is where her journey begins.

EMILY'S

Angie staggers through her kicked in front door and picks up the phone in the hallway. Tentatively sitting on the settee in the front room, as she was hurting all over, she rang the police. When connected to an officer, she burst out crying.

"Hello, I am PC Constable Smith here, how can we help you?"

"Please, can you come here to my home ASAP? Something horrible happened to me when I was out this evening. I have just got home." Angie took a while to say this between sobbing, stuttering and her hands and knees shaking.

He asked for her address and said, "Angie, stay right where you are, we will be there in 10 minutes. In the meantime, barricade yourself in your bedroom."

"Okay thank you, please hurry I am so terrified."

After the call, she slowly went upstairs, phone in her hand and into the bathroom. She washed her hands and face, suddenly vomiting into the basin. Going into her bedroom, she moved what furniture she could up against the door. Then sitting on the bed rang her best friend.

"Hi, Jane sorry calling so late, can you please stay on the phone for a while, till the police get here?"

"Hi Angie, shit, what's happened, my friend? Of course, I will."

Angie said what she could remember, which was scant while sobbing.

"Okay, now please take some slow deep breaths, it will help to calm your nerves."

"I'll waffle on about work so that you feel confident knowing I am here, okay."

Angie muttered, "mmm."

They both heard a squad car with sirens blaring, then a voice shouting "It's okay Miss Angie Brown, it's the met police here, we are coming up; is that okay?"

Angie yelled, "yes."

She moved the furniture from the door, and three cops entered. Then picking up the phone said, "oh, thank you, Jane, they are here. I will be okay, my friend."

Jane replied "I'm coming over. I'll be there soon, pet."

After many questions, to which she answered the best to her knowledge, it was advised that they take her to A and E to see a doctor.

"No need officers, I am okay," she stuttered in between sobbing.

"No, Miss Brown, we don't think so; you are in shock, plus your knee is wounded. It won't take long for a doctor to check you over."

Minutes later, Jane arrived and off they all went to the local hospital. She was examined and advised to remain as an in-patient for at least a day.

It transpired that her drink had been spiked by an ex-boyfriend who had tried to drag her into his car. That was the reason her clothes were torn, and a fight had ensued. Little did he know that after buying her a drink at the nightclub, she had taken a few sips then ditched it when he went to the bathroom, as she had an appointment mid-morning at the gym and was looking forward to it.

Since their breakup a year ago she had taken up kickboxing as self-defence, after being slapped and punched by him. It was also a stress buster and fitness exercise. Well, fight she did and survived to tell the tale. As for her front door being kicked in, that was part of his vindictive revenge at being rejected by her. Thanks to a CCTV camera in the car park near the night club, he was photographed with her beside his car and thankfully arrested two days later.

SKY'S

I should not have had all the shots. I can barely stand. Luckily, I'm not drunk enough to not know what I'm doing. The worst part is my tights now have small splits, and my new shoes rub. I love them shoes. I search around my bag for my keys, I see messages on my phone from James offering to take me home, but I didn't want him to worry. We've only been together for three months. Great now the phone battery is dead. They just don't last long anymore, not like the old days. Ah, there they are! As I'm just about to unlock my door I see it has been completely kicked in. I freeze. I cannot move nor speak. Who would do this? I'm all alone and defenceless. An intruder is in my house; I need to go in. I creep up to my doorway; I silently and cautiously push my crippled door ajar. How it's still on its hinges is a miracle in itself.

Just. Silence.

I haven't made a noise so far. Whoever is in there would still be unaware of my presence. At least I have the upper hand. Blood trails are all over the wooden floors, handprints on the walls. It looks like a fight took place here. My sofas have been rearranged, pictures on my mantlepiece have smashed, or the image has changed.

The curtains to my garden are drawn, what's going on? I avoid all the creeks in my floorboards as I know where they are. Outside in my garden, a shovel sticks in the ground... wait... that's a grave! I let out a gasp, which was not going to help me now; whoever is here knows I'm here now.

I turn to run. The look in his bloodshot eyes is enough to give me nightmares forever. Blood smeared on his face, is it even his?

"Take a seat," he whispers. That voice. I can't speak. He repeats himself, but this time he wasn't so polite.

"Take...a... seat!" He throws me to my sofa, the sofa pushing well back. He sits opposite me; he moved our chairs so we would be facing each other. Everything is off, the radio I always leave on when I go out, just to let strangers know a presence is in the house. The phone lines have been cut. The room so silent you'd hear a pin drop.

"What are you doing here Mike?" The ex-boyfriend I thought I'd never see again. He left me for someone else a year ago.

"I'm here to see you."

"Quite the dramatic way, even by your standards."

"I want you back." He looks in my eyes. His voice is as if he is struggling to speak.

"You're the one who left me, remember?" He wasn't fazed by the heartbreak he left me with.

"I made a mistake; now I'm back."

I cannot believe I'm hearing this. Oh, so because he left and it didn't work out, I have to sit and wait for him?

"No, it doesn't work that way. I've moved on."

He leisurely carves shapes in my sofa with the knife.

"So I see," he says as he continues to carve.

I search for a weapon or even a quick escape. I can't escape. He'd outrun me easily. Everything I could use is out of reach. I'm trapped.

"Who's that in my garden?" my voice cracks as I ask the question.

He looks to the window and then back to the knife.

"The man who's ruining everything," he responds coldly and tears well in my eyes.

"Is he...?" My god, I hope he hasn't.

"He's fine; he's still alive... for now. He's just gonna be very dirty when he wakes up."

"This isn't right, Mike. This is all wrong! I'm getting James, and we're leaving..."

He stares up at me. "Who said you're leaving..."

DANNY'S PROMPT

A FAMILY RETURNS HOME FROM A WINTER HOLIDAY TO FIND A DEAD BODY IN THE PARENT'S BED. THE WEAPON USED IS A POGO STICK. THE HOME PHONE LINE AND MOBILE LINE ARE BOTH DEAD.

ABOUT DANNY

Danny left our group when he moved from the area, but he still visits us on occasions when he comes back to see his family.

DANNY'S

Back To The House

A family came home from a winter holiday to discover a dead body in the parent's bed, and the weapon used was a pogo stick, the landline and mobile phone lines were dead.

Doctor Emmett Brown was the first person to enter the bedroom; the kids Jules and Verne were being entertained by Clara in the living room. Emmett could hear lots of laughing from downstairs while he stared in horror at what laid before him.

Blood was everywhere; it was splattered all over the walls and the floor. Emmett slowly walked alongside the bed, and as he got closer to the body, he covered his nose and mouth with a handkerchief to try and stop the hideous smell invading his nose and mouth. He tried to make out who the victim was, but the face was so brutally caved in by the pogo stick what was left of the victim's face was unrecognisable.

Emmett started to feel like he was going to be sick, so he turned and walked to the bedroom door. He turned his head around looked at the body then lowered his head and walked out of the bedroom closing the door behind him. Emmett stood outside the door for a few seconds to gather his thoughts and to try and think of a way of telling Clara and the boys that they couldn't stay at this house anymore, without worrying them, as well as trying to keep Clara from going into their bedroom. He had a look at his watch; the time was 10:04 pm on November 5th, 2085.

Emmett said in hushed tones, "Great Scott!" At first, he thought could that body be a future relative of Biff Tannen or even Marty McFly?

As if from nowhere Clara appeared at the top of the stairs and by Emmett's face, she knew straight away that something was wrong. The fear in his eyes as well as the look of how pale his face had become.

"Honey?" she said obviously concerned, "what's the matter? It looks like you have seen a ghost."

She ran over to him and hugged him so tightly and whispered in his ear "Whatever has spooked you it will be alright, I promise."

At that point, tears started streaming down his face, and he said in a croaky voice, "I don't think it will be, but promise me one thing, never go into our bedroom again."

"Why?" she said.

"Because you love me, and I never want anyone of us ever going back in that bedroom." He tried to lead her to the stairs, but she got away from him, and as she was getting closer to the door there was a loud BANG! Clara collapsed to the floor. She was dead instantly. Then another BANG! Emmett fell to the floor dead.

Verne came running up the stairs to see what all the noise was about then BANG! The force of the bullets made Verne completely miss the stairs, and he collapsed at the bottom; dead.

To Be Continued........

BAILEY'S

The family that I'm the servant of returned home to my little gift. The father of the family paid me extra to guard their much-loved house in their absence, and I really needed the money but, little did Mr Brixton know that I knew his deep dark secret and while they were away, I may have made it harder to keep. But, don't go thinking that they are a family of sinners because young Miss Amber Brixton (their only child) has a heart of gold. She's the only reason why I continued to work for them, to see her grow up happy fills my heart with joy.

Let's move on to my surprise for their return. As a loyal servant is expected to do, I did guard their precious home, and that's how I saw the intruder enter through the back-garden gate, expertly picking the lock. Out of sheer panic, I reacted in the only way I could think of. I had to do it. I had to. I grabbed hold of the object nearest me; Miss Amber's pogo stick and swung. I felt the connection with the back of her head, and I instantly knew I had hit too hard. Even after serving in the army, I'm still not used to having blood on my hands, yet there I was again laced with guilt from my unlawful act. Almost as a second thought, I turned the body over to expose the face of my victim, and that's how I decided what to do next. With all the strength I could muster, I lifted the body and carried it to the master bedroom and put her to rest where she's meant to be.

And with that, I left a simple note that read: 'I protected your house, but you're the real monsters. And all this time I thought she was dead…' and I left the house without another look back.

I know they won't share my surprise; they will keep it hidden as best as they can. I guess it's just another secret under their belt. I'm entirely sure of this for the victim was, in fact, Miss Amber's birth mother.

VICKI'S

"Kids wake up; we're home," Danny shouted over his shoulder as he drove up their driveway.

"Thank goodness," Kate, his wife said as she stretched out her arms. "That drive felt never-ending!"

They got out of the car, the two children, Colin and Isabella, slower as they were sleepy.

Kate was the first to approach the front door, and as she neared, she stopped so abruptly that Colin walked into her.

"Danny!" She shouted in such a fearful tone that everyone immediately knew something was wrong.

The front door was ajar; the broken lock was laying on the floor. Danny gingerly approached; he yelled a "hello" wanting to give anyone inside the chance to leave. He had no intention of confronting anyone while he had his family there.

As he slowly pushed the door, he jumped as Kate touched him on his shoulder.

"Sorry." She whispered, "There's no mobile reception to call the police; I need to use the house phone."

"No reception?" Danny asked, confused. "We usually have good reception here."

"Well, we haven't now!"

"Okay, walk behind me," Danny said as they made their way to the kitchen where the landline was located.

"Damn! That line is dead too." Kate whispered. "What is going on?"

"There doesn't seem to be anyone downstairs; nothing has been disturbed. Strange. Lock yourself in the car with the kids while I check out upstairs."

"No chance! Wait here while I get the kids into the car and I'll come too."

Danny mulled it over and decided that the extra pair of eyes was probably a good idea, plus he wasn't feeling as brave as he was portraying.

A few minutes later and the two of them were creeping up the stairs, cringing when one of the stairs creaked.

The bathroom door and both kid's bedroom doors were closed as they had been left, but the master bedroom door was fully open.

They cautiously approached the room, and they both came to an abrupt halt when they saw what was inside.

A naked man was laying on their bed, his arms and legs were splayed so that he looked like a star, and his eyes were wide open. But what really drew their eyes was Isabella's pogo stick was standing upright out from the man's chest. Judging by the amount of blood and the gaping holes in his torso, it had been rammed into him several times.

As one they turned and ran out of the bedroom. Kate tripped on a stair in her haste to get down them, but luckily Danny caught and steadied her. They didn't even worry about pulling the front door closed as they left, they just wanted to get away and put as much distance as quickly as possible between them and their house.

From the master bedroom window, a figure watched them leave.

"That's a shame they are back," he said regretfully to the dead man, "I hadn't finished with you yet."

KEV'S

Pogo'ed

A family return from a winter holiday
to find a dead body in the parent's bed.
The weapon used was a pogo stick
the home and mobile lines are both dead.

Who is this lifeless body in their bed?
and how did she get there?
Holes pogo'ed into her torso
she was straddled across the bed bare.

Is the killer still loose in the house
if they are where can they be?
Sticking together the family search
from room to room to see.

The house was silently empty
but the garage needed to be checked.
Upon opening the side door
they saw the garage totally wrecked.

By the shut garage door
standing straight up was a pogo stick.
Moving slowly, closest to the smallest child
as if he knew who to pick.

The family ran off in different directions
all yelling and screaming.
Pogo stick bounced after them
Handle looked as if it was beaming.

Mother ran towards the bedroom
but she had no idea as to why.
She locked the bedroom door
and kneeled down and began to cry.

Father ran fast into the kitchen
grabbing the biggest, sharpest knife.
He crept back down the hallway
Looking for his children and wife.

The youngest child a girl
Locked herself away in the bathroom.
Child number one a boy
Went sprawling while grabbing a broom.

Father called out quietly to his family
creeping along in the dark so slow.
As he peeped around the corner
Pogo jumped up and gave him a blow.

The boy came running and shouting
waving high, his broom now broke.
Pogo just bounced from side to side
And leapt in the air ready to poke.

A towel came from out of nowhere
and Pogo was now covered in the dark.
It fell to the floor and was being sliced
which was beginning to leave a mark.

Mother was sitting on one end
a hammer denting the pogo stick.
Father was at the other end
knife in hand, ready to end it quick.

He started to unscrew the pogo's feet
and take away his flying ability.
When he finished his family sighed
relieved by the chance of tranquility.

He unscrewed the pogo stick entirely
putting it away in a chest.
Sitting down with kids and wife
he sat back for a welcomed rest.

They went back to see the body
and found a bag of jewelry and cash.
Pogo had killed a burglar
they realised together in a flash.

JONATHAN'S

Person A: "It's nice to get away, but it's good to return to normality. All that mountain climbing was very tiring. I could do with a rest."

B: "I'll be up later."

A: "There's a big man in our bed. There are brown and red stains all over the place, and the man is oblivious to my screams."

When the bedclothes were removed, it was obvious that the man was dead. He had lost a lot of blood, and his teeth were smashed. A pogo stick was lying on the floor.

A: "I wonder if the killer used the pogo stick to break the man's teeth. But who is he and why is he here?"

The television announcer said, "Strongino the Strong Man is missing from the Chadwell Heath Circus."

B: "I knew his face was familiar. We should call the police. There's nothing the ambulance service can do for Strongino."

The phone line was dead, and the mobile phone had to be recharged.

Person C: "Strongino wasn't very popular, and it seems that he had financial problems. There have been several burglaries in the area. In each case, the burglar has wrenched open the windows of properties that were considered impregnable."

Person D: "But he's such a big man. He couldn't have entered the bedroom unaided."

C: "He must have lifted an accomplice through the window. That person would have opened the front door for him."

D: "That makes sense, but how did Strongino receive his severe internal injuries?"

C: "I still think someone used the pogo stick to smash Strongino's teeth in."

D: "But that doesn't explain the ruptured intestines and the massive hiatus hernia or tumour by the diaphragm."

C: "These X-rays are more revealing. They remind me of the death of Edward II, who had a red-hot poker thrust up his backside. In this case, the pogo stick was used to go in through the outdoor. The stick ruptured the organs as it passed through the alimentary canal and out through the mouth. The forensic reports are consistent with the bodily fluids found on the pogo stick."

D: "How did Strongino cope with that?"

C: "Well, he had a very strong constitution, which is probably no surprise, and managed to get into the bed before he died."

D: "But how did the pogo stick enter Strongino's body?"

C: "Take a closer look at the tumour. Do you remember the disappearance of Pingo the dwarf? He must have been Stongino's accomplice, but they argued. He used the pogo stick to enter Strongino's body but was dislodged as he passed through the diaphragm."

MARK'S

They're all six feet under; it's done; the pogo killer had killed my last family member. They are avenged, and now I'm sitting on the edge of the world thinking about life. My life; my new life, that awaited me down there in the city. It's so peaceful at night; hiding the sin behind a dark blanket. All I see in the dark are the faces of the men that I have killed, and I wonder, did I do the right thing? Did all the monsters that I have murdered in their name make me one too? Would I have a line of people waiting to find me for the same reason that I hunted them? Who knew? All I knew is that in a few minutes they might get their wish.

Jenny has suspected me since we went to that house because she said I knew my way around well, and from then on I was being watched and taken off the case because of lack of results, they said. I agreed and let them get on with it. I knew who was next and took them out quick. They are searching for clues across the street to me, searching for phantom clues which I know are not there. The new life I wanted I could no longer have as if I left now it would be too fishy. So, I made the call to dispatch that I was chasing the killer on the roof and that's when Jenny arrived all 'gung-ho'. I shot her in both kneecaps, and I picked up her gun and shot myself in the shoulder. I had a smoke while she bled out, then I passed out from blood loss.

I awoke two days later in a nearby hospital, and I hear how they found the evidence that I had planted. I hear about how Jenny was the killer and how she was unstable. She died from my shots; I explain how I didn't want that but had taken one in the shoulder and passed out. They ate it up; believed it all, as I hoped.

When I got out of the hospital, I quit the force; personal reasons. Jenny was my friend, and I killed her. Just an excuse, I murdered loads of men, all with a pogo stick. I got the new life I wanted, and I visit Jenny from time to time to say sorry, it helps you know.

So, if you find this letter, this is my confession, that I Detective Kate Malone is the pogo killer, not Detective Jenny Forrest.

I sign the letter and put it in my journal. What a journey I have been on! It had to be written somewhere and where better than my journal. Will it ever be read? Who knows? My new life awaits- the pogo killer is retired.

EMILY'S

Returning home after three weeks on a Winters sports holiday in Switzerland the Jackson family were tired yet elated about their experience. It was their first visit to Switzerland plus a first for Winter sports activities.

However, little did they know what lay ahead when they entered their home jet-lagged. Tired emotionally and physically within a couple of hours, they were all exhausted.

The police had been called, an ambulance had come and gone, and quite frankly it was chaos. So many questions asked and so many answers to be found. Only time would tell how and why this living nightmare had occurred.

It all began with a scream from Mrs Jackson when she entered her bedroom with some luggage.

Mr. Jackson ran upstairs, shouting, "What's wrong, Sue?" As he went into the room, he gasped and put his arms around his wife's shoulders.

"Oh my God," he uttered as they both trembled.

There on their bed sprawled out and covered in blood lay a middle-aged man; a complete stranger. Adam moved closer to see if the person was alive. He felt his pulse; there was none.

He picked up the phone to call 999 but couldn't as the line was dead.

"Sue, let's get out of here to call 999." By now, their two teenagers, Maggie and Tom, were in the doorway witnessing the gruesome scene. They all went downstairs and out the front door and knocked at the neighbour, George's, door. Thankfully he was at home. He smiled and was about to welcome them home and ask about their holiday. However, one look at their faces told him something was wrong.

On hearing what had happened, he ushered them in and here they stayed waiting for the police and ambulance to arrive. The children were sobbing uncontrollably. Sue was crying and shivering. George brewed tea, adding sugar while chatting to Adam. No, he had not heard anything from their house while they were away. Though he had been staying at his sister's home for the past four days arriving back that morning; it was now late afternoon.

When the police arrived, they asked Adam to go with them back into his home. Of course, he was reluctant, but had to go.

With slow deep breathing, he turned to Sue, saying, "You stay here love with the kids. I will bring our suitcases and whatever else I can think of back here. No way are we setting foot in there again."

"Ok, love," she muttered.

When in his bedroom he saw a bloodied pogo stick being removed from under the bed and wrapped up by an officer. He remembered it was a birthday gift to his daughter Maggie two years ago from himself and Sue. Tears fell from his eyes, his hands were shaking, and his knees were wobbling.

He returned to George's house and his family.

From that day on the house was unlived in and eventually demolished by property agents as no buyer could be found after the story hit the headlines.

It remained an open case with the police.

SKY'S

I'm so glad to be home
from our winter holiday break,
there's only so much snow
my boots could shake.

Unpacking our suitcase
home from the cold,
the weather has been nice here
so I've been told.

Mum was in for a shock
when she checked her bed,
a body lay tucked in
sticking out was the head.

Shocked to the core
she let out a yelp,
we dropped our belongings
and ran to help.

Who is this woman?
How did she get in?
By the looks of her death
she went with a grin.

A blood trail leads
from the bedroom to the hall,
the mess all over the floor
even all along the wall.

There lays the weapon
the dreaded pogo stick,
not the first weapon of choice
when it's lying next to a brick.

She broke our window
the glass completely smashed,
blood on the edges
she clearly had something slashed.

Rummaging through our belongings
throwing the pogo on the floor,
constantly in her way
she threw it to the door.

The rubber of the stick
bounced off the door,
knocking her in the face
falling to the floor.

Her nose starts to bleed
bested by a pogo stick,
she started to wrestle it
then beat it with a broomstick.

As the stick lay bent
she had clearly won,
now back to business
there's robbing to be done.

She took what she wanted
and left to run,
tripping on the stick
feet in the air as she spun.

Knocking her head
she felt herself fading,
killed by a pogo stick
how degrading.

KATHY'S

Back from their skiing holiday, the first thing they saw was the pogo stick strewn across the hall floor.

"Which one of you left that lying there?" shouted Dan.

"Not us, dad," chorused the twins in unison.

As Amy bent to retrieve the stick, she felt a sticky substance on her hands. "It's blood," she cried dropping it to the floor.

"Don't be stupid," said Dan as he made his way up to the bedroom with the cases.

The body was lying on their bed. Dark red blood seeping from the wound in her neck onto the pristine white sheet. Stifling the cry that threatened to erupt from his lips, he grabbed his mobile phone from his pocket. No signal. He picked up the landline. Dead. Fear shot through him as he moved towards the door.

"Keep calm, don't let the boys hear," he whispered to Amy. "I can't explain now, but we must get out of here. I think our lives are in danger. There's a corpse in our bed, and the phone lines are dead we must get out."

As they turned to go, Amy stared at the bloody pogo stick still lying on the hall floor.

I am stepping out into the darkness a plaintiff howling pierced the cold night air. They stood transfixed as the sound moved towards them. As the boys began to scream hysterically Dan gently ushered them towards the car.

Without warning a tall thin woman appeared through the gloom. "It's okay, don't be frightened, I mean you no harm, but we must get to the car quickly. We are in grave danger."

"Who are you, and what are you doing here?" asked Dan.

"Something or someone has been terrorising and killing people in the neighbourhood. I managed to get out of my house when we heard someone break-in, but my husband was not so lucky."

"What happened?" sobbed Amy, but the woman could give no rational explanation. All she could say was that she had found her husband dead on the floor, a bloody pogo stick lying across his body.

As Dan turned the ignition, the car refused to start. Panic gripped him. Before he could try again, the sound of heavy footsteps approached. They watched in horror as the door handle slowly turned.

When they were found police said they had never before seen such fear on the face of a dead person.

'Pogo stick killer strikes again' read the headlines in the Daily News.

The death of a young family and an unidentified woman found in Ealing Broadway yesterday, the latest in a line of similar killings in London is causing severe problems for the Metropolitan Police who have yet to identify a motive for these brutal attacks. The only clue a note the perpetrator leaves beside the victim. 'Beware the pogo stick killer'. The Metropolitan Police Commissioner today appealed for help from the public. This person must be found before any other innocent people suffer. If you have any information, please call Scotland Yard in confidence.

HANNAH'S PROMPT

THE HOUSE WAS NOT WHAT IT SEEMED.

ABOUT HANNAH

Hannah was a valued member of our group and is still missed. She set off on a new adventure in another country to teach English.

HANNAH'S

An ancestral family home needs a new tenant. The house has been in the family for centuries but due to numinous circumstances, requires a new lease on life.

It's a beautiful detached four-bedroom house situated between the emotive cliffs of Redrum and the edges of Gallows Moor. Only a stone's throw away from the town but far enough away from prying eyes and curious people who never heeded the story of the cat.

This late Victorian home will make a perfect new beginning for a single person who wishes to escape the humdrum of city living or just wanting to escape.

Excellent sound-proofing so you won't have to worry about the harsh winds and voices disturbing your restful sleep.

The house has a conservatory allowing perfect views of the rolling seas, that seem to beckon you into its embrace, and a spacious garden just waiting to be treated with love and care. There is a sensitive rock bed, so digging below six feet is not recommended.

As expected with old houses, it's important to separate the truth from wife's tales. One such regarding a family of five who were believed to have been butchered in their living room and the bloodstains are visible even today. There are no such bloodstains as all the floorboards have been replaced with a rich, dark oak.

There is no basement and please do not attempt to look for one.

Please respond promptly if you wish to become a tenant. We promise the house will be everything you have ever wanted and will offer things you never expected.

We accept cash payments.

Smokers and liars need not apply.

No dogs, they worry the animal on the moor.

Contact: Lucius Von Boucher III.

BAILEY'S

Usually, I wake up in bed with birds chirping at my windowpane and my cat nudging me awake with her wet nose — not today. I woke up to me being carried towards a small yellow house and a sick feeling in my stomach. The house itself looked well-kept and but the hands that held me were rough and aggressive which caused me to wonder.

I tried to break free from the unfriendly grasp as my thoughts faded into blackness. Once again, I awoke, this time to silence and a sharp pain in the back of my head. I sat up to see a room full of light. It reflected off the white walls, wooden floors and white equipment and cupboards and the bright bed on which I sat on. Lastly, there were two white wooden doors, and just as I began to plan my escape, one of the doors abruptly opened.

"Good morning Jane, there's no need to worry. I saw you were injured, so I brought you home."

I remembered an accident, and although the room did feel secure, I had a feeling that this man was too prepared for me.

The tall, ambiguous man smiled, "The others can't wait to meet you. You're home now."

And then all went black.

Report:
Wednesday 11th July 2018.
Chris Wright arrested at 24 Church Lane.
House seemed innocent.
A neighbour phoned in talking about an abnormal amount of activity taking place in the yellow house.
Seventeen young girls and women were found in small rooms, some pregnant, all physically unharmed. Each woman recalled a car accident and then waking up in a medical room that Wright had set up in a spare room.
Charges:
Kidnapping.
Assault.
Rape.

VICKI'S

Jerry stood and stretched his back. He took pride in the appearance of his house. The paintwork looked white, the windows and curtains were clean, and the garden neat and tidy.

He was about to get back to weeding when he heard the voices of his elderly neighbours approaching. They spent a few minutes exchanging the usual pleasantries. He couldn't help but smile as they headed off as he overheard their parting comments:

"Such a nice man! His wife was mad to leave him!"

Jerry finished weeding and smiled, pleased with his work. Perfect house, from the outside at least, but this house was not what it seemed.

The difference between the out and inside was noticeable immediately on entering. In every room, the wallpaper was old, faded and had small holes. The paintwork was sun-bleached and covered in grime, dents and chips. The furniture was old and shabby. The place hadn't had a clean in months. Dust, coffee stains and half-eaten food covered the surfaces.

One room in the house was in an even worse state, and that was where Jerry headed. Taking a key out of his pocket, he unlocked the door and went inside. The curtains were drawn, but the darkness didn't matter, he already knew where she was sitting.

Chained to the wall and sitting on a dirty mattress sat a woman. She raised her head as he entered, and her greasy, unkempt hair fell from her face. She looked at her captor with helpless dead eyes. She had long ago given up hope, the man that she had once loved was no longer there; this cold hard stranger had replaced him.

"The outside world thinks that you left me, that I'm the victim," Jerry sneered at his wife, "you don't exist anymore!"

KEV'S

"This old house is supposed to be haunted. Apparently, nobody has been in there for years. Skeletons are supposedly laid out in the different rooms," whispered Garry as they stood outside the front porch.

"Well, I'm going through the Orange door and see for myself," said Mike Barrett.

"I'm knocking," Mike continued. There was no answer, so he quietly turned the handle and the door slowly opened.

Bright light oozed from every corner of the large room. To the two young men, it was very inviting.

They walked in wearily. There was a very tall grandfather clock in one corner with a rainbow of colours running around it. A stunning corner unit of soft suede went all around the room, and in the middle was a coffee table with drinks of all types and cakes and sweets. Music was silently coming out the walls; it was not music they had heard before.

They sat down and proceeded to enjoy their new surroundings. Laughter echoed around the house as the two boys reminisced over stories they had heard about this place. All so untrue.

The house was not what it seemed.

Mike and Garry had been in a severe car accident, and both were critical in intensive care.

Doctors had advised their parents to expect the worse.

JONATHAN'S

I was in the house of my dreams. The owner, Miss Patterson, grimaced as I described each room before we entered it. I mentioned the chandeliers and walk-in wardrobe. Miss Patterson didn't need to persuade me to buy the house. I thought she'd be happy to have such an appreciative buyer, but she looked unhappy as we reached the front door.

"Is anything wrong? This is a lovely house."

"It was lovely until the guests arrived. I couldn't cope with them, so I had to sell it."

"Who are the guests? I thought you lived alone."

"They appear occasionally, but only one really scares me."

"Who is this person?"

"I'm afraid it's you."

That concept disturbed me, but I had lived with myself all my life, so I felt I had nothing to worry about. I bought the house and enjoyed living there for several years. I could cope with strange noises at night but was upset by children crying, as if they were being beaten.

I contacted "Haunt Hunts", and my house appeared on the television programme. My neighbours complained about sleepless nights due to the strange sounds which were becoming louder. They contacted the council, and the staff members were sympathetic until they found small bone fragments between some floorboards. The police discovered children's skeletons and the screams became even louder.

After the police investigations, the council decided to destroy the house so the neighbourhood could return to normality. I didn't want to leave my other self. I am in my front room watching the wreckers arrive and stop.

People are shouting, "Where is the house? It was here a moment ago."

I am safe for now.

KATHY'S

The house stood on the hill, empty and desolate since the fire had reduced the once beautiful property into the sad building it now was. Time had erased memories of the tragedy of the twins' death; life had moved on, and the gossip about whether the house would be inhabited again had ceased.

Katie had always loved the house, drawn there despite her mother's warnings never to go near it. As a child she had slipped out exploring the overgrown garden, climbing through the gap in the broken shutters. Wandering around the empty rooms, she felt a sense of belonging; the house seems to whisper to her 'I am not what I seem'. I was once a happy house filled with laughter and fun, not sad and empty."

Katie never understood why her mother became so angry when she went to the house.

As she wandered up to the house one day, Katie was taken aback. A tall thin woman was painting the front door, long strokes of cobalt blue shining bright against the disappearing brown background.

"Hi there," said Katie.

The woman turned around to smile when her face turned ashen white; the brush dropped from her hand as she staggered back, "Get away from me," she cried.

Katie turned and ran back home. "Mum, come there's a strange woman at the old house. She shouted and frightened me."

Katie's mum approached the house - her worst fears confirmed as she watched the woman walk inside. She had never dreamt she would return; never thought she would see her again.

She clutched Katie tightly to her and with a heavy heart moved slowly back down the hill. The woman had seen Katie; it was only a matter of time before the secret would be revealed. There was nothing she could do but wait.

MARK'S

The house was old really old, but it had more to it than you would know; if you only would peak inside. It has many rooms and many doors of all different colours, shapes and sizes; some for adult, some for children and even some for dogs.

The house was maybe left by a magic man or an alien, nobody knows for sure, all they know is if you enter you never return. But why is this? Well, you see the doors lead to different points in your life; some happy, some sad. You can even see loved ones again, or maybe guide yourself to a different path. But what you don't know when you enter, is that it takes a terrible price for using a door; you become a door yourself.

So if in your neighbourhood you see a house that looks old, run-down, grey and in need of more than a lick of paint; and you decide to peek inside, if you see doors from wall to wall, some big, some small, some brown and some red. Remember my tale and the price you will pay. You will see the ones you love again or take a new path, but that will no longer be you. You will be a way for another to do these things. Will you end up back at the house? Well that is for you to find out someday!!

EMILY'S

From outside the house was not what it seemed as semi-detached in a quiet suburban road. For five years now it was a haven for like-minded people - all down to Jane, who with a huge lottery win and had bought it. Her own house was next door.

She was very excited about her plans as now retired, and up for a challenge, it was financially possible. The house had been on the market for Nine Months when she put in an offer to buy at less than the asking price as she knew the owners wanted rid of it. It was holding up their plans elsewhere. Her offer of the cash up front was accepted immediately. Three bedrooms, two reception rooms, kitchen, bathroom, two toilets plus an annexe out back in a large garden. It was the beginning of her new venture.

Sharing her plans with family and friends offers of regular help was offered by those like her retired.

Six Months later painted furnished throughout it was officially opened.

Now, reader, you want to know, a haven for like-minded people, what is it all about? Well after consultations with her Doctor and police checks on her carried out and cleared, she was warmly received to continue her non- profit-making Community Project.

Monday to Friday: 10 am to 12noon and 2 pm to 4 pm

Activities were held in every room. Yoga, Writing, Art, Drama, and Music in the annexe out the back. Clients with depression, anxiety, social phobia were referred by their GPs It was welcomed by all and a huge success. Jane was very proud of her achievement. Never too late, all is possible, was her motto.

The icing on the cake was a Government Grant awarded for one year to cover expenses re tutoring, heating, refreshments etc. with the opportunity to apply again the following year.

SKY'S

"Split up!" Aaron screamed at his friends. Three policemen chased the three ten-year-old boys into the forest. The adrenaline rushed through Joshua as he sprinted through bushes and branches, cutting his knees and arms. He hides near a rock to gather himself. Typical that his shoelaces become loose. No time to tie them up. As he turns, he sees a house surround by trees. The green vines wrap around it, looks as though it's holding it in place.

"Stop right there!" The policeman has Josh in his sights.

'No, not now!' he thought. He has to chance it. Josh dashes through the shrubs, leaps up the stairs and flings his body at the door, tripping on his shoelaces on his way in. He Slams the door shut and leans against the door catching his breath.

"What are you doing here boy?" a gruff voice shouted at him. The old figure was holding his broom ready to use as a weapon.

"I'm just hiding sir, don't hand me over please."

"What did you do?" he questioned.

Josh was very reluctant to answer, but he knows the old man will hand him over if he doesn't.

"Me and my friends egged our teachers' house."

The old man rolled his eyes. "If you're gonna commit a crime at least make it a good one." Josh will remember that.

Josh leans forward to tie his laces only to see poison ivy vines have double knotted them for him. The cuts on his knees and arms now had plasters on them. Josh decides to wait by the window.

"Oh no he's coming!" Josh screeched.

"Just relax!" The old man snapped. The policeman walked towards them still oblivious to the house. He walked through the stairs leading up to the door and straight through the house? How? He searched high and low for the boy who stood a few inches in front of him but couldn't see him.

"Can you see 'em?" he shouted to his colleagues.

"No, keep looking." The cop continued forward walking through the walls of the house.

"I think they're gone," Josh whispers.

"Good. Now scram!" Josh didn't want to stick around, so dashed to the door. He jumped the three steps and into freedom.

"Where did you go, Josh? We were looking for you everywhere," his friends asked.

"I hid in the house with some creepy old dude." Aaron and Mike raised their brows.

"What house?"

"That... house?" As Joshua turned to point to the house, that was no-where to be seen.

CESAR'S PROMPT

THE LAST MOMENTS
OR
HE LIKED TO WATCH HER AS SHE SLEPT

ABOUT CESAR

Cesar left our group when he managed to find employment. He did, however, try his best to confuse us as he decided to set two prompts, allowing us to choose which one we wanted to use for inspiration.

JONATHAN'S

I'm a man just happy to see you sleep

Bob: Tanya has been so unhappy recently. I have tried so much to make her feel wanted, but to no avail. Her childhood traumas keep coming back to haunt her; from being locked in a cupboard, being beaten for not coming first in exams and being assaulted, physically and mentally.

When she can get to sleep, she often cries out in agony. It horrifies me to hear her pain. Is it worse for her to have nightmares or to suffer from insomnia? All this is affecting her work and making her irritable. She has been given a final written warning about her behaviour. One more case of verbal abuse and she's out and how will we cope then? At the moment, we can only just afford the rent. Her managers say that they have done all they can to help her, but to no avail. Customers have made a lot of complaints and fewer people are visiting the office. Profits are down, and Tanya can't really expect to be kept on if she is losing money for the company.

The doctor has given Tanya some new medication, and it seems to be working. She looks so peaceful as she lies on our bed: no snoring, no screaming, no attempts to get up and raid the fridge.

I'm just happy to see you sleep, Tanya. I hope that you can overcome your demons, whether I have caused any of them or not.

Tanya: I watch Bob looking over me as I sleep. He has been so kind to me. I'm so glad he still wants to be with me after all I've put him through. I know I've hurt him so much and many men would have left me by now.

He is still here and still wanting to be with me. I need someone like him after the way I've treated him so badly. I can only hope I can help him in the years to come.

MARK'S

I hold her hand in the last moments. The illness slowly eats away at her until the end, and as I touch her hand, I see the life we had; the laughs, the children we had and all that brought. Now it's her last moments, and I'm sad she's spending them alone. She was there with me during my last moments, and now I'm here for her, but she can't see me.

I've waited for her here for so long it seems. I hold her hand and say, "I love you," and she smiles.

"Can you hear me, my love?" I ask to which she replies, "I can always hear you, you silly man. I'll be with you soon." Her eyes shut, and suddenly she's standing next to me, and I cuddle her, and we leave her last moments. We are off now to our next adventure.

I hold his hand in his last moments, a stranger. I've no idea who he is, but I don't want to let him die alone. I wonder what life he had. Children? A wife? Now it's his last moments, and I'm here with him keeping him company. Who will be here for mine? Will I meet that man of my dreams I hear about and will he sit with me? It's a journey I am yet to have; I will have to wait and see. The man grips my hand and says, 'thank you', then his eyes close and he's gone. Off to his own adventure, to what comes next and I'm off on mine.

These are the last moments; one of many. What will yours be and who will be with you? Your journey starts now!!

EMILY'S

It was a warm sunny day in March, which was unusual for that time of year. Alice decided to sit in her garden after replenishing the bird stand. She was admiring the garden while formulating in her mind a story to write. It was of an experience years ago that she had. Pen poised and just about to start she spotted Kitty her cat jumping over the fence. As she was climbing down a tree trunk, Alice noticed something sticking out of her mouth. Thinking it was a twig with a leaf attached, she thought no more of it.

Until, wait for it reader, as she approached, Alice realised what it was. There was movement around Kitty's mouth. Have you guessed the reason?

It was a tiny mouse, yes! A live mouse. Kitty ambled passed the garden table and plonked herself on the grass behind Alice's and began meowing. It went through Alice's mind to try and save the mouse, the little creature. However, a memory of years back popped into her mind. Her cat Toby had walked into the kitchen from the door which led to the garden, with a live bird in its mouth. She had immediately leapt to the bird's rescue to be hissed at furiously by Toby. Who then ran out to the garden with the bird still in its mouth?

So no, she wasn't going to chance a repeat performance like that. With her legs up on the chair beside her, feeling yuk, helpless and cowardly, she said sorry in her mind to the mouse and wished it a speedy demise.

Just then, the phone rang. It was her daughter, "Hi Mummy, how are you?"

"Fine thanks, my love and you?"

"All good my end Mummy, any news?"

"Well yes, Kitty is sitting behind me with a live mouse, I can't bear to look."

"Ah, that's nice she has brought you a present, she will be alright."

"It's not her I am thinking about; I know she is okay."

After the call, Kitty ambled past the table, minus the mouse. Taking slow deep breaths, Alice went to look where Kitty had sat with the mouse. Wait for it reader there's more. No sign of a mouse, although the grass was relatively long. Was it there? No way was she going to poke around. If it appeared, it was half alive or deceased, and neither was she brave enough to see. Or maybe just maybe she thought, it had run off after Kitty was tired playing with it?

Alice was informed that her daughters' cat actually ate mice. Oh, it was just to yuk to investigate. Mice were not a pleasant sight for Alice under any circumstances. Alice said to nobody but herself, as by now, Kitty had wandered off, 'A present? Well, a bunch of flowers or a box of chocolates from family or friends is very nice indeed. But a frigging mouse from Kitty? Thanks, but no thanks, my little friend. Keep those presents well out of my sight, please.'

She truly hoped the little mouse had got away to live another day or more, as she went indoors to make a cup of coffee, before sitting down to watch some comedy sketches and unwind.

So that's it folks, a different story from the one I had planned. The best-laid plans and all that ha, ha.

SKY'S

Dear Diary,

It's been a while since I wrote to you, but with so much going on I guess I never had time to write. Or maybe I was too scared to write in case I started crying. I still can't process what has happened. Something happened recently. I have never felt so powerless in my life and can't help feeling it's my entire fault. This was his last moments.

"Have you spoken to your mother, Tom?" I asked him.

He turns his head to face me, with the look of, "I think you already know the answer."

"Of course, I haven't. I've no idea where she is." I look at his pale complexion. He is just skin and bone now. He really did lose his way, because of me.

Tom lost his way, and I wasn't there when he needed me the most. Me and his mother divorced a few years ago, but that isn't why he got hooked on drugs and alcohol. His mother Jane was a recovering alcoholic, well I say recovering, she tried for years to stop but just didn't have the will power. She was violent towards me one night, and that was the final straw. I packed my bags and was ready to leave. I tried to convince Tom to leave with me, but he loved his mother too much to leave her, he always thought he could save her, but the truth is he was never safe with her. But I left him. The look on his face when I picked up my bags and slammed the door behind me still haunts me now. There isn't a day that goes by where I wished I could turn back time and made him come with me. On Wednesday 11th, Jane phoned me at 1:45 am drunk as a skunk shouting that she hasn't seen Tom for two days. I couldn't believe what I was hearing. Two days! What has she been doing?!? Don't worry I already know the answer. I drove around endlessly, searching parks, the streets, stations. But nothing. My phone rang, and it was Tom.

"Tom, where are you?"

"Hello sir, I'm sorry but I've found a body in the alley behind Martin's corner, he's still breathing I've called an ambulance, and they're on their way."

I couldn't breathe. I couldn't speak. I put my foot down to his location. I see an older woman leaning next to him keeping him warm. I ran over to him screaming his name, and I see his nose is broken and surrounded by whiskey bottles. I just hold him. The ambulance arrives, and we're now on our way to the hospital. I tried ringing Jane but surprise surprise no answer. He's been in there a while; I'm now panicking.

I'll never forget those heart-breaking words the doctor told me as he leaves the room Tom was in.

"I'm sorry sir; his liver has sustained too much damage. He won't make the weekend; we'll do everything to make him comfortable."

"I just want to sleep, dad."

"I won't stop you from napping Tom. I'll be more than happy just sitting here."

"No." He looks up at me. "I mean I want to sleep," he replied as his voice cracked.

I just couldn't wrap my head around what he was saying until it finally hit me. He shouldn't be saying this. He's only twenty-three years old with his whole life ahead of him.

My head drops on the arm of his chair. I didn't bother fighting back the tears; they were going to stream either way.

"I failed you, Thomas. I am so sorry."

"No, you didn't fail me. I don't want to be in pain anymore. It's time," he whispers to me. I hold his hand tighter, and the tears overflow from my eyes. He looks at me, but I can't return the eye contact. He clutches my hand back.

"I can't remember the last time I even slept. Just be happy that I'm finally going to." His grip on my hand loosens... then drops. I raise my head to look up at him. His eyes are closed. Tears stream down his cheeks and fall to his shirt. For the first time in weeks, he's finally asleep. I release my clutch on his sweaty palms, and I kiss his forehead one last time.

"Goodbye, my son."

I rise to my feet and make my way to the door, rubbing away the tears from my eyes. I open the squeaky door and wave to the nurses for their attention. They know the worst has happened. I take one last look back at my son, lying peacefully in the hospital bed. I am a man. I am a father; who feels happy to see you sleep.

BAILEY'S

To the love of my life,

I hope that you've had a good day at work and that your meeting went well as I know you were nervous. I was just sitting here remembering our first date all them years ago now. It was at that romantic restaurant, do you remember? You got me a bunch of beautiful pink tulips (my favourite of course) which we then had at our wedding. Oh…our wedding how marvellous it was. We danced and sang and drank and loved. A day I'll treasure forever. Looking back now, I can clearly see how that night was our last moment of true happiness as married life wasn't something you can ever get used to, but I can only see that in hindsight.

You see, my love, I felt as though our love was dying, so I knew I needed to act. Before your big presentation last week I came by your office to give you a tulip and wish you good luck, and when I finally navigated my way through the maze of white walls and brown doors I happened to stumble upon…well, I think you can guess what I saw, and that was my last moment of faith in us, in you. After that day I played the part of the perfect, unknowing wife and I believe that you never noticed that I was just there, hovering, waiting until I could leave as I still had to wait, not only for some papers but for my heart to give up – spoiler alert it still hasn't.

Which leads to today my dear, I can't move on while I'm still holding on and unlike you, I can't "love" two people at once. Today the key to my release arrived, I have signed them, and I'm praying you will too as if you ever loved me this is your chance to prove it – set me free. I will keep you in my prayers, and I hope you live a good life full of joy and love.

Love,
Your now ex-wife.

P.S I left my keys on the side (by the toaster), and there's some dinner in the fridge, heat it in the microwave; 8 minutes should do. Now I really must go. Goodbye.

VICKI'S

I had two last moments with you mum.
Both are still firmly etched on my mind.
Moments never to be forgotten but to be cherished, and to be feared.
They gave me love, hope, anger, helplessness, joy and sadness.
Such a range of emotions,
And such opposites!
So how did I have two last moments?
Here's how:

My first, last moment with you was the last time I saw you alive.
Discharged from the hospital on a Wednesday,
No hope left; the end was near.
You lay in bed,
A shadow of your former self.
Refusing food; only water passed your lips.
After a few days, you stopped talking,
It was an effort for you to even open your eyes.
Visitors all day,
Sadness all evening,
Tears all night.
A week went by; Tuesday at bedtime.
I'd spent a few hours sitting by your bedside watching you as you slept,

Finally, exhausted, I got up to head to bed.
As I got to the door, as I always did, I said: "Goodnight, love you."
You surprised me by answering, "I love you too."
You lifted me,
You gave me false hope!
After not speaking for days, I heard your voice,
You had improved, I thought,
You were fighting again, I thought.
I didn't know I'd never hear your voice again.
I didn't know my heart was about to break.
I didn't know you would pass away peacefully that night.
Because if I had, I would have treasured those last moments with you.

My last, last moment with you was the hardest of my life.
I sat beside your bedside, holding your lifeless hand in mine.
The doctor had been,
Made it official.
It didn't seem real; it still doesn't.
I didn't want them to come and take you away.
Everyone said their goodbye's and I could hear them downstairs,
But I couldn't leave you alone in your bedroom,
Waiting to be taken away.
I didn't have any tears to cry,
They came later in great big gasping sobs that hurt my whole body.
Instead, I sat holding your hand,
Letting you know you are loved.
It doesn't hit me then that a giant hole had begun to appear,
A hole that will never be filled.
We only have one mum in life, and you can never be replaced.

I wish my last moment never had to end,
But it did.
Watching them take you away was soul-destroying, heartbreaking, the end.

Time has now passed,
But you are not forgotten.
You are still loved.
You are still missed.
Every memory is cherished and shared.
And I know, somehow, that you are looking out for us still,
After all, a mum is a mum forever.

GISELLE'S PROMPT

ONCE UPON A TIME IN WONDERLAND.

ABOUT GISELLE

Giselle left the group just after setting her prompt.

JONATHAN'S

Once upon a time in Wonderland

Many creatures say that narcolepsy is a curse, but it can be a blessing. A girl called Alice has just complained that my friends used me as a pillow while I slept. She didn't ask me how I felt about it. At least I was being useful, and that can be a problem when I spend most of my time asleep or am I awake? I can't tell the difference.

Alice is now complaining about the unbirthday party. Why? I don't know when my birthday is or if I've ever been awake to celebrate it. At least I can have a good time if I'm awake, if that I be. At least the hatter and hare want me to be there. Why did Charlie call them mad? They just look at the world in a different way, and surely, they have the same right to their opinions as the rest of us. They could be right in a world where so many things are wrong, and it is always safer to agree with others, rather than being an antagonist, whatever that means. I'm so tired I don't want to think about it. Why should I?

Alice is such a hypocrite. She seemed bothered about me having tea poured on my nose or being used as a cushion, but she liked beating time, as if it were time's fault that she was hyperactive and couldn't relax or whatever. Beating time wasn't a problem, but murdering was. How could you murder time? Do I do that when I sleep? "Twinkle, twinkle little bat." Bats live longer because they sleep more, so how could they murder time? Surely, they prolong it, as, perhaps, do I?

How did Elsie, Lacie and Tillie appreciate time when they lived at the bottom of a well and couldn't see the moon or Sun? Those celestial bodies were much farther away than the sisters were to the well's entrance. The girls could draw treacle in more ways than one. The exhibition of 'Treacle Art beginning with the letter M' never made it to an art gallery, but, like a crashing tree, it doesn't mean that it never existed, whatever that means.

I feel tired again. Thinking exhausts me, and I don't know if I'm awake or asleep. My friends are trying to put me into the teapot so that I can sleep unmolested.

At least I'm unlikely to get into hot water again while I'm asleep. Can my dreams hurt me?

MARK'S

Once upon a time in wonderland, well, it was that in name only, most wonder how they got there. Dirty streets filled with homeless men and women, not poor, just have nowhere to go. The main centre is now part of a game where six enter but only one leaves. There are just too many people, so they do this to lower the population.

Today was the turn of Steven Smith and five others. He felt sorry for them as he was a trained killer, while they were all bank clerks and shop workers. One by one, they fell to him and his blade. The last alive was a young girl, and he sees her there, all scared and looking death in the face. He gives her his blade and says, 'Do it!' She kills him but little did Steve know that the real game was about to begin.

He awoke in a strange bed, the world outside looked like it did in pictures. The sky was blue; he had never seen a blue one or breathed in such fresh air. There's a machine on his bed, the name 'death hint 2389' was written on it. Was it all just a game? He was confused; his real-life must be a sad one. Was Steve really his name? He had no idea until he looked in a mirror and if he was a Steve, then it was a lady Steve, as a blonde, middle-aged women looked back at him! This was all a mess!

'Wonderland', the sign read outside her house- new game from the makers of 'death hint 2389'. She sees a box on the desk, and it said, 'Wonderland', but that was not what she had played. She examines the computer and understands that Steve is her avatar. She doesn't know why her memory is gone, and she goes to her balcony and sits there and has a cigarette and waits for her memories to return. They don't; after she smokes, there is a blinding light, and she is in a hospital bed; once again, she is Steve. Why? How?

The young girl that he had spared is there holding his hand.

"He's awake," she booms, and a flood of people appear.

"You are one of the few," a doctor said. Steve doesn't know who he is! The women or himself?

With a puzzled look, he asks, "The few what?" After forty minutes of explaining from the doctor about how as he had spared a life, he had been given some time in the old world. How it was before, 'a rare privilege,' they said.

"Who was that women?" he asked. The women replied that it was her mother, but Steve was not a nice man and sold the secret to the other world and had lived like a king. No more street sleep for him. As for the young girl, she also sold it but used the money to build a big home for the homeless people, and she never saw Steve again.

EMILY'S

It was not long ago that life was so very different. What are a few thousand years in the bigger scheme of things? You reader may be thinking different, how different?

Well, let's get started with nowadays, shall we? Towns are overcrowded with people and buildings. Noise is twenty-four seven in most places. The working day is no longer nine to five for many people. Many businesses work twenty-four seven with people on a shift system. Three shifts a day. A person may be on one, two or all three a week or fortnightly. Let's face it, reader, it's a non-stop world we live in mainly.

As you read on, just imagine how different it used to be as I give you a snippet of life a different way.

Once upon a time in Wonderland, people lived in villages. Each was self-sufficient growing their own crops. Leadership came from the elders who met up weekly to discuss local affairs. Fortnightly everyone within a village would gather with the elders to share any woes and concerns. It was a democratic debate where everyone had the right to their own opinion and were encouraged to speak up.

With guidance from the elder's resolutions were always found in a caring, compassionate manner. If at any time an individual was aggressive, going against the village and the good of all, then it was a period of rehabilitation or the choice to leave the place forever.

This seldom happened where a person chose to be evicted, as life in other villages was similar. Voluntary leaving one's own village occurred when a female would marry and go to live in her husband's village. No one was forced, and all was amicable. Each place had its own medicine man a Shaman along with nursing aides in a long wooden built building.

This was a time before money was invented; people helped each other willingly. Every three months, Elders from neighbouring villages would gather together to discuss any concerns and updates of village life. While a formal agenda for the smooth running of village life was necessary, the fundamental law was 'Love and Care for All; Without Question'.

From birth till death, everyone was catered for. There was no such word as loneliness as it never occurred. If a person chose to live on their own in a tepee or wooden hut, there was always help at hand if needed.

It was a hunter-gatherer way of life. Women gathering crops, nuts berries etc. Men are hunting for meat. Before a hunt, prayers would be said to God for protection along their way. Prayers to the animals were given as an apology before their slaughter; it was a natural way of life. Animals hunted another animal, and people hunted animals for survival. However, people carried this out in as quick and humanely as possible way.

Everyone and everything were treated with respect. Where services were rendered an exchange in the form of help was given where possible. Fortnightly the inhabitants of a village would gather together in the open when the weather was fine or in a purpose-built wooden lodge. Each would bring food and drink to share with all.

So, to you the reader, I have given a snippet of life in a different way. Once upon a time in Wonderland. Were you able to envisage it? I know I was as I penned my tale, I also know in the blink of my eyes which time of life I would choose.

How about you?

BAILEY'S

Once upon a time in Wonderland, the sun rises like it always does, lighting up the World of Good with oranges and pinks. The land has a mixture of establishments, from cabins to toadstools to castles. The world's bell tolls to signify the start of a new day upon the crime-free land. Everything glitters and glows as the inhabitants emerge from their homes to enjoy their days of happiness. If you look closely you can see some of your favourites roam around the town centre. There's the boy with the scar scratched across his forehead or the boy who found the golden ticket. You can find a beautiful girl with metres of golden hair hanging out her tower as she sings her "Good mornings". If you're lucky, you'll be able to see the group of unlikely friends skipping arm in arm down the yellow road.

It's a world of peace, a world of harmony.

Across from this world lies another that's the opposite, it's surrounded by gloom. The inhabitants thrive in this darkness as it matches the darkness within themselves. Here there are no laws, so chaos runs free. There's no day, only night as that's when they feel at home. Not only would you find the violent criminals, such as the dark lord and his loyal companions, but you'll see the doctors who make potions or create monsters as they too are full of darkness. If you listen carefully, you can hear the cackle of laughter that acts as a warning before they zoom over your head on battered broomsticks. This could be a place full of your nightmares unless this sounds like a dream to you.

There's one last world within this solar system. The Forgotten. It's the one that when you remember it, it brings you pain and sorrow. This world too is dark, but the inhabitants aren't as happy. They are waiting for the day that they can be reunited with their loved ones again. The world is a graveyard full of the ones we have lost. A wife or a husband. A dear old House Elf. Lonely, they wait. The only way they can reunite is when the author decides it's the right time. However, many authors are long gone, and many sequels go untold, leaving them lonely forever.

VICKI'S

Once upon a time in wonderland,
A king looked out to survey his land,
His soldiers paraded to honour their king,
Followed behind were the ladies who sing,
Their songs of all of his heroic deeds,
And how he cares for his citizen's needs.

His daughter looked out from her tower so high,
She too watches the parade as it passes on by,
She puts on a dress and places on her crown,
Studies her reflection; perfection; and heads on down,
To the Great Hall where they are holding a feast,
Looking forward to sup on the big cooking beast.

A knight watched her enter; his heart skipped a beat,
His cheeks went bright red, and he shuffled his feet,
This knight is known as the bravest in the land,
But he can't make eye contact; he just stares at his hand,
Instead, he turns away and talks to a nearby wench,
And his heart breaks slowly as they sit on a bench.

A servant girl rushes around the castle with care,
So many jobs to get done, don't slow down, she doesn't dare!
A thrashing for every job that she doesn't complete,
Ensures that she keeps moving, she's rushed off her feet,
She serves the knights at their tables with a dread,
Wanting the long day to finish, she wants her bed.

After a long day of festivities, the king heads to his room,
Alone and unhappy, he'd mastered his own doom,
By murdering his wife, the love of his life,
By mistakenly accusing her, he pulled out a knife,
And before he knew it, she lay dead at his feet,
Keeping the truth from his daughter was a tough feat.

The Princess too was in her room all alone,
Her stomach clenched and let out a small moan,
As she knew that soon a stranger would suggest marriage,
To unite pure bloodlines, so she'd be put in a carriage,
And expected to start a new life far away,
She felt like a possession, to be used, castaway.

The knight was now full of wine and strong beer,
He looks the wench in the eyes, realises he has nothing to fear,
As she smiles at him shyly, he pushes all thoughts aside,
And decides that he needs just to forget his pride,
Because this pretty young girl could be just what he needs,

To come home to after fighting and performing great deeds.

The servant girl now with jobs done for the day,
Heads home to her family runs quick all the way,
As she wants to see her children before bed,
And hug them tight and kiss them lightly on their head,
Her husband will tell her to sit down and relax,
While he recounts of his day with his usual wisecracks.

So, who is the happiest in this magnificent Wonderland?

The king with his power but no love in his life?
The Princess waiting to become a stranger's wife?
The knight who has decided to give love a go?
Or the servant girl whose home life makes her smile and glow?

KEV'S

Spiderwebs and rust residing together in harmony
There's Death and destruction everywhere you look
And the silence is abundant in its own absence
Time has come and stolen life like a wizened crook

Groaning machinery aching for a mighty stretch
Creaking noises occasionally feed the dank air
Now stood empty and desolate with false hope
A place where thousands came to a stop to stare

Colour evasive upon entering its gates ever again
Even in the sun, the wasteland palate was very dull
Tents drooping in the rain-drenched soggy ground
A moment when the humans had their last cull

This place used to be full of colour and brightness
People enjoying themselves in the atmosphere
laughing and giggling lifted up high in the sunlit day
oblivious of what their limited lives should fear

Humans brought about the demise of the earth
With hate and bile bringing nothing but war after war
Killing mother nature and then killing themselves
Nobody knowing ever what it was actually for

And now there is nobody left to come to this park
To bring creation back to cover and destroy the bland
Regenerate this wonderous, exciting creative fair
Once upon a time in wonderland

Lightning Source UK Ltd.
Milton Keynes UK
UKHW010633250821
389444UK00002B/387